FREE STYLE SCRAPS 04
GIRLIE

Published by BNN, Inc.
11F Shinjuku Square Tower Building
6-22-1 Nishishinjuku Shinjuku-ku
Tokyo 163-1111
Mail: info@bnn.co.jp

Edited & Designed by 4D2A, Sayaka Ishii

Translated by R.I.C. Publication Asia Co., Inc.

ISBN 978-4-86100-534-3

Printed in Japan by Shinano, Ltd.

FREE STYLE SCRAPS 04 GIRLIE　ライセンス契約書

1. ライセンス

1) 株式会社ビー・エヌ・エヌ新社（以下「弊社」という。）は、本製品を購入され、本ライセンス契約書記載の条件に合意されたお客様（以下「ユーザー」という。）に対し、本ソフトウェアを同時に１台のコンピュータ上でのみ使用できる、譲渡不能の非独占的権利を許諾します。

2) ユーザーは、2 の「制限事由」に該当する場合を除き、本ソフトウェアに含まれる素材を加工・編集し、もしくは他の素材と組み合わせるなどして、主に以下のデザインに使用することができます。

○ WEB などのデジタルメディア ○店舗の内装、案内表示などのグラフィックツール ○印刷物として頒布するチラシ、フライヤー、ポスター、DM、カタログ、パンフレットなどの広告・販売促進ツール ○個人制作・個人利用の雑貨、服、グリーティングカード、名刺など

(個人的・職業的・商業的用途の利用を認めますが、いずれも非売品のデザインに限ります。個人においても素材を利用した制作物の販売は行えません。また、書籍や雑誌など売品の印刷メディアに素材を利用する場合は、使用の範囲によって別途料金が発生する場合があります。右記連絡先までお問い合わせください。MAIL : info@4d2a.com / TEL : 03-3770-2807 / FAX : 03-3770-2807）

次の制限事由をよくお読み下さい。

2. 制限事由

以下の行為を禁止します。

1) 本ソフトウェアを１台のコンピュータで使用する為のやむを得ぬ場合を除き、本ソフトウェアを複製すること

2) 本ライセンス契約書に基づくライセンスを他に譲渡し、本製品の貸与もしくはその他の方法で本ソフトウェアを他者に使用させること

3) 流通を目的とした商品のデザインに素材を利用すること

4) 著作権者に無断で、書籍や雑誌など売品の印刷メディアに素材を利用すること

5) 素材を利用してポストカード、名刺、雑貨などの制作販売または制作サービスを行うこと

6) 素材を利用してインターネットによるダウンロードサービスを行うこと（グリーティングカード・サービスを含む）

7) 素材をホームページ上で公開する場合に、オリジナルデータがダウンロード可能となる環境を作ること

8) ソフトウェア製品等を製造・販売するために素材を流用すること

9) 素材そのものや素材を用いた制作物について意匠権などの権利を取得すること

10) 素材を公序良俗に反する目的、誹謗・中傷目的で利用すること

3. 著作権、その他の知的財産権

本ソフトウェアおよび素材に関する著作権、その他の知的財産権は、弊社または弊社への供給者の排他的財産として留保されています。素材を利用した制作物においてユーザーの著作権を明示する場合は、素材の著作権「©Miyuki Matsuo」「©Machiko Ito」「© Omoko Okamoto」「©eto」を併記してください。

4. 責任の制限

弊社および弊社への供給者は、請求原因の如何を問わず、本ソフトウェアの使用または使用の不能および素材の利用から生じるすべての損害や不利益（利益の逸失およびデータの損壊を含む。）につき、一切責任を負わないものとします。

5. 使用許諾の終了

ユーザーが本ライセンス契約書に違反した場合、弊社は、本ライセンス契約書に基づくユーザーのライセンスを終了させることができます。

FREE STYLE SCRAPS 04 GIRLIE License Agreement of the Software

1. License

1) This License Agreement is a legal agreement between you (the "User"), who purchased the product FREE STYLE SCRAPS 04 GIRLIE, and BNN, Inc. ("BNN"), in respect of the attached CD-ROM entitled FREE STYLE SCRAPS 04 GIRLIE ("Software"). The User agrees to be bound by the terms of this License Agreement by installing, copying, or using the Software. BNN grants the User the right to use a copy of the Software on one personal computer for the exclusive use of the User.

2) The User may modify, edit, or combine the materials included in the Software except the cases specified in "2. Limitations"; the User has the right to use the Software principally for design of the following objects.

○ Digital media including websites.

○ Graphics for shop interiors, signs, etc.

○ Leaflets, flyers, posters, direct mail, catalogues, pamphlets, and other tools for advertisement or sales promotion.

○ Goods, clothes, greeting cards, name cards and other articles for personal production and use.

(The Software may be used for personal, professional, and commercial purposes, provided that the articles produced are not offered for sale. If the software is used to design products for distribution including books and magazines, a copyright fee may occur according to the scale of use. You must contact the copyright holder. MAIL : info@4d2a.com / TEL : 03-3770-2807 / FAX : 03-3770-2807)

Please read the following Limitations carefully.

2. Limitations

The User is not licensed to do any of the following:

1) Copy the Software, unless copying it is unavoidable to enable it to be used on one personal computer.

2) License, or otherwise by any means permit, any other person to use the Software.

3) Use the Software to design of products for distribution.

4) Design of products for distribution including books and magazines without asking copyright holder.

5) Use the Software for the commercial production of postcards, name cards, or any other articles, or sell any such articles made using the Software.

6) Provide downloading services using the Software (including greeting card services).

7) Create an environment which allows the original data to be downloaded when you show one of the Software patterns on a home page.

8) Use the Software in order to produce any software or other products for sale.

9) Acquire the copyright in any material in the Software or any object you have created using the Software.

10) Use the Software to create obscene, scandalous, abusive or slanderous works.

3. Copyright and other intellectual property

BNN or its suppliers reserves the copyright and other intellectual property rights in the Software. When specifying the User's copyright of a product made using the Software, please also write "©Miyuki Matsuo", "©Machiko Ito", "©Omoko Okamoto", "© eto".

4. Exclusion of damages

In no event shall BNN be liable for any damages whatsoever (including but not limited to, damages for loss of profit or loss of data) related to the use or inability to use of the Software or use of materials in the Software.

5. Termination of this License Agreement

If the User breaches this License Agreement, BNN has the right to withdraw the User's License granted on the basis hereof.

CD-ROM をご使用になる前に

○注意すること

●必ず P.002 のライセンス契約書をお読みください。
● Mac OS X（10.4.8）、Adobe Photoshop CS2、Adobe Illustrator CS2、Windows XP で動作確認済みですが、環境が異なる場合や、操作方法が分からないときは、OS やソフトウェアに則した、お手持ちの説明書をお読みください。

○準備

まずは CD-ROM をセットして、「FSS_04」フォルダを開きます。必要なデータをピックアップし、デスクトップにコピーしましょう。「FSS_04」フォルダには「JPEG」と「EPS」という 2 つのフォルダが入っています。

○データの種類

掲載したすべてのイラストレーションは、それぞれ JPEG と EPS の 2 つの形式でファイルを用意しています。（データはすべてモノクロになっています。EPS ファイルは、Illustrator のバージョン 8.0 で保存しています。）

JPEG

JPEG ファイルとして収録したのは、350dpi（商業印刷に耐え得る解像度）に設定したときに、掲載サイズと等倍の印刷面積を持つビットマップ画像。「Adobe Photoshop」をはじめとするビットマップ系のソフトウェアで編集できるほか、多くのソフトウェアで扱うことが可能です。

EPS

EPS ファイルとして収録したのは、拡大縮小を行っても画質が劣化しない、ベクトル画像。ドロー系のソフトウェア「Adobe Illustrator」でファイルを開くと、自由にカスタマイズできます。（ビットマップ系のソフトウェア「Adobe Photoshop」で開くと、「ラスタライズ」という工程を経て、ビットマップイメージに展開します。）

○データの見つけ方

JPEG データは、下の図のようにページごとにナンバリングされています。（たとえば 018 ページの場合「p018_1.jpg」「p018_2.jpg」「p018_3.jpg」「p018_4.jpg」「p018_5.jpg」、019 ページの場合「p019_1.jpg」「p019_2.jpg」「p019_3.jpg」「p019_4.jpg」というファイル名で収録されています。）EPS データは 10 ページ単位で 1 ファイルとなっています。（たとえば 020 ページから 029 ページまでは「p020_029.eps」というファイル名で収録されています。）

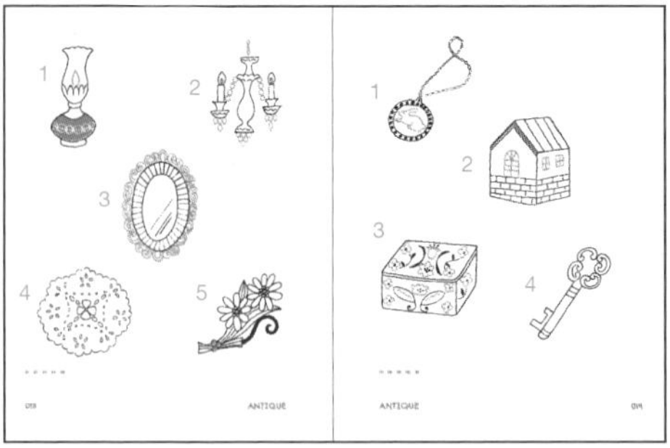

Before you start using the CD-ROM

○ Notes

● Please read the conditions of use on page 003.

● The functionality has been verified with Mac OS X 10.4.8 , Adobe Photoshop CS2, Adobe Illustrator CS2, and Windows XP Professional SP1. If your system is different, or if you have a question concerning the operation of the software, refer to the manuals corresponding to your OS and software.

○ Preparation

Set the CD-ROM and open the folder "FSS_04". Copy the folders you need onto your desktop. There are two folders in "FSS_04" : "JPEG" and "EPS".

○ Different kinds of data

All the illustration in the book are prepared in the following two formats:

※ In the JPEG file, you will find bitmap images which are printed on the same size as shown in the book at 350 dpi the resolution suitable for commercial printing . You can edit them with Adobe Photoshop and other bitmap software, and you can use it with many other types of software.

※ In the EPS file, you will find vector images, which do not deteriorate when you increase or reduce the size. Open the file with Adobe Illustrator or other drawing software, and you will be able to customize the images freely. When you open the file with bitmap software such as Adobe Photoshop, the image will be developed as a bitmap image after the process called rasterizing. (EPS files are saved with Illustrator 8.0.)

○ How to find the data

As for the JPEG data, the illustrations in each page are numbered from top left as shown below. For example, the illustrations on page 018 are named "p018_1.jpg", "p018_2.jpg", "p018_3.jpg", "p018_4.jpg", "p018_5.jpg"; as for page 019, "p019_1.jpg", "p019_2.jpg", "p019_3.jpg", "p019_4.jpg".

As for the EPS data, there is a file for ten pages. For example, all the illustrations on pages 020 to 029 are found in the file "p020_029.eps".

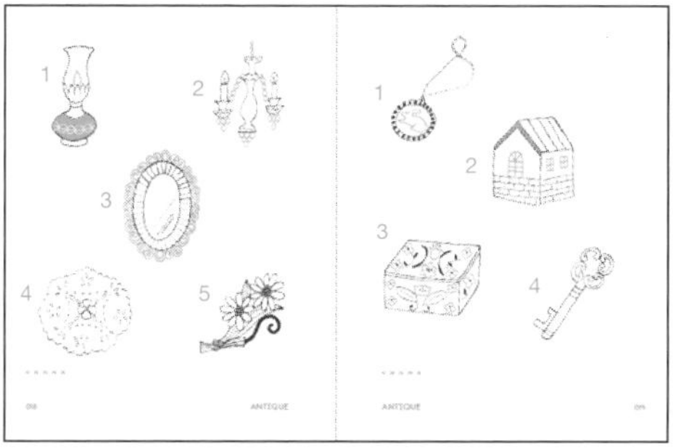

EXAMPLE

いつでもどこでもデザインやレイアウトがしたい。
これは、そんなあなたのための素材集です。プレゼンテーションやウェブ制作の現場、ビジネス、また生活のさまざまな場面で役立つよう、幅広いテーマから素材を選び、それぞれ1000点以上のイラストレーションを収録しています。また、誰でも簡単に利用できるよう、掲載したイラストレーションのすべてを、付属するCD-ROMに汎用性の高いJPEG形式と、Adobe Illustratorのベジェデータとして扱えるEPS形式で収録しています。

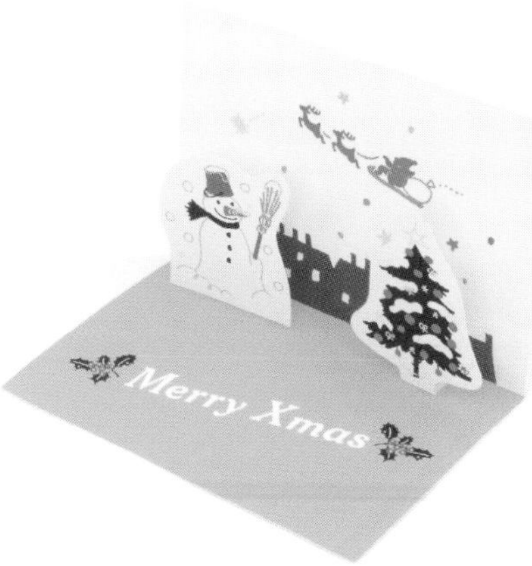

「クリスマスカード」コンピューター上で好みの絵柄をカードサイズに配置し、厚紙に印刷。年賀状や誕生日カードなど、各種のオリジナルカードが作れます。

「エコバッグ」熱転写紙使用。インクジェットプリンタで鏡像印刷し、家庭用のアイロンでプレス。Tシャツにも転用できます。

Christmas Cards: Arrange your favorite designs with your computer and then print it out onto postcards. You can make your original New Year cards or birthday cards.

Eco Bags: You will need "iron-on transfer paper" to do this. Using an inkjet printer, print out your design onto the transfer paper. Next, iron this onto the fabric of your choice. You can make an original T-shirt in the same way.

Want to arrange and layout a design anywhere and anytime? -then this collection of designs is for you. With over 1000 illustrations from a wide range of themes this design package is sure to meet your various purposes - from presentations, website designs, business needs to everyday uses. To make it user friendly, the attached CD-ROM contains all the illustrations in JPEG file format and EPS file format for Bezier curves of Adobe Illustrator.

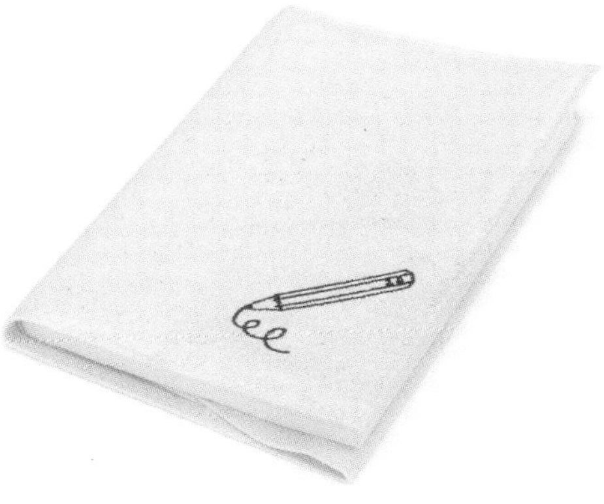

「ブックカバー」ブックカバーの布に絵柄をトレースし、手縫いで刺繍。刺繍機能付コンピューターミシンを使えば、あっという間に可愛らしい刺繍が楽しめます。

「マグカップ」出力サービス業者に委託。データをメールで送ってから１週間で完成。１点からの注文も可能です。

Book Jackets : Trace your favorite illustration onto fabric and embroider along the lines. If you use a computerized sewing machine with embroidering functions, you will have fun making lovely designs in no time.

Mugs : Just send your originally arranged design data to a specialized manufacturer, your original mug will be ready in a week . Orders can be placed for as little as one item.

FREE STYLE SCRAPS 04
GIRLIE

INDEX

01 02 03 04 05

01 02 03 04 05

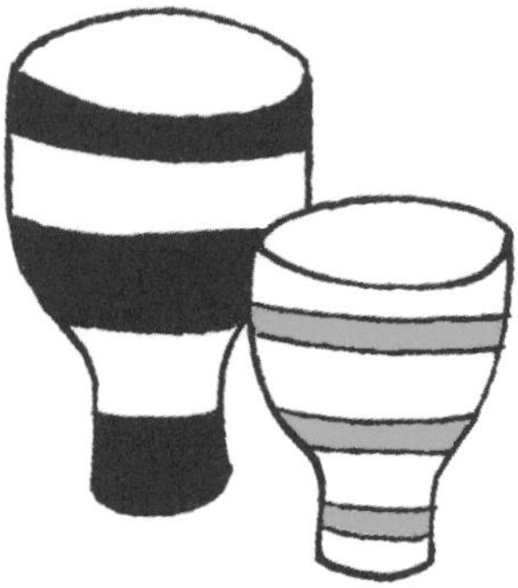

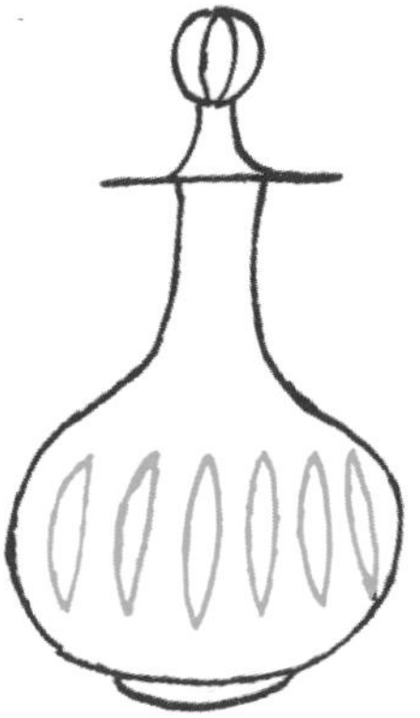

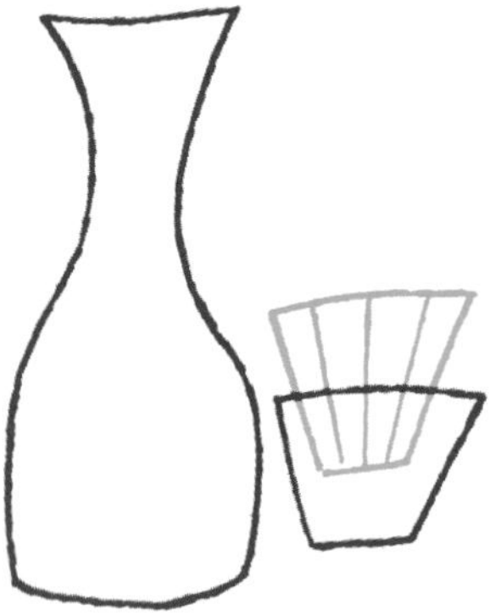

01 02 03 04 05

01 02 03 04 05

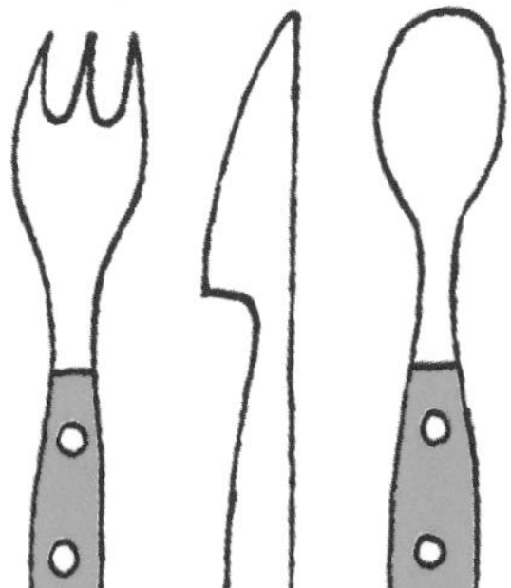

01 02 03 04 05

01 02 03 04 05

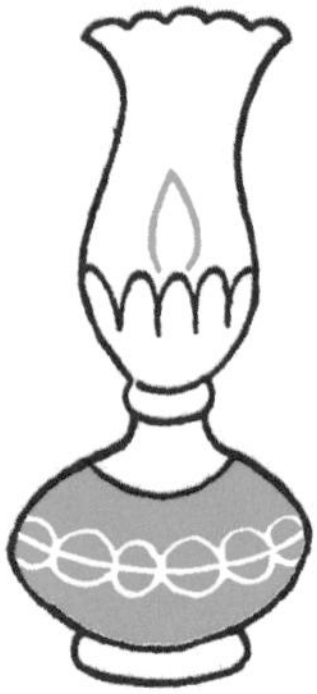

01 02 03 04 05

01 02 03 04

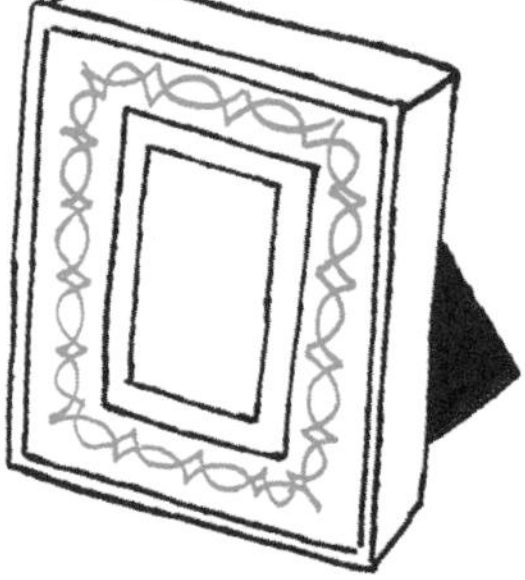

01 02 03 04

01 02 03 04

01 02 03 04 05

01 02 03 04 05

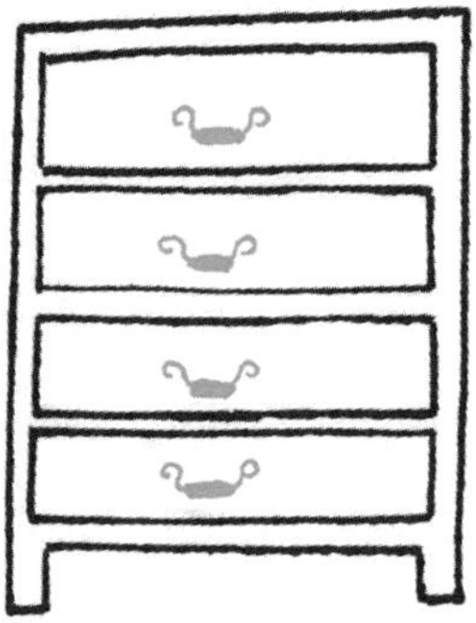

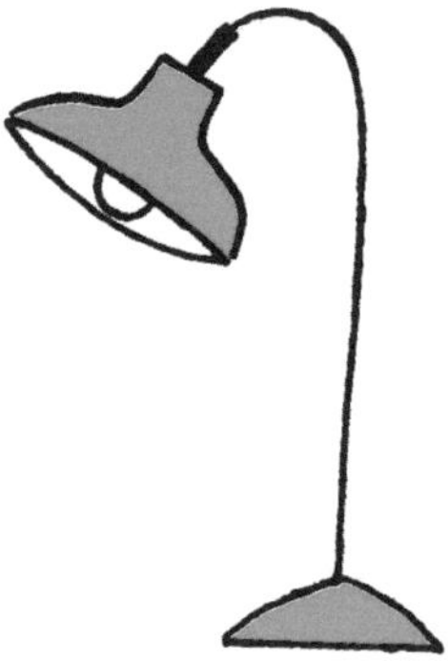

01 02 03 04 05

01 02 03 04 05

01 02 03 04 05

01 02 03 04 05

body
milk

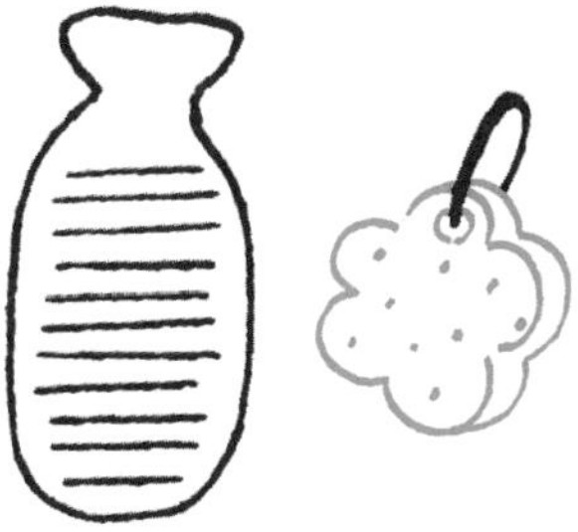

01 02 03 04 05

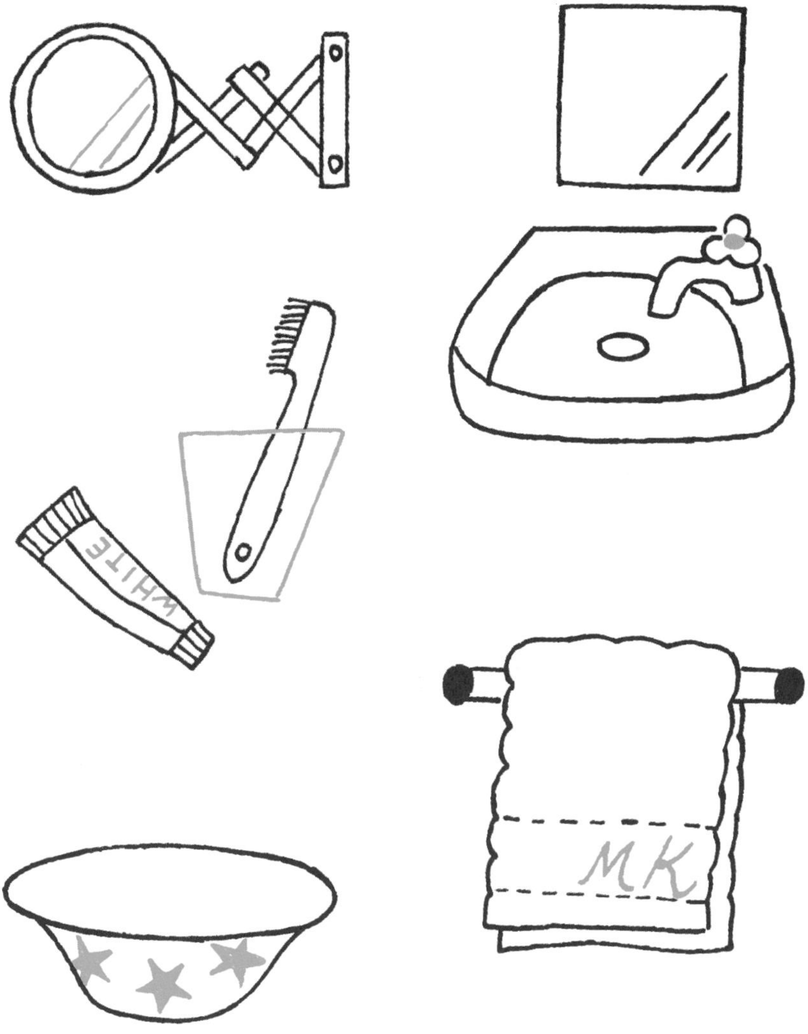

01 02 03 04 05

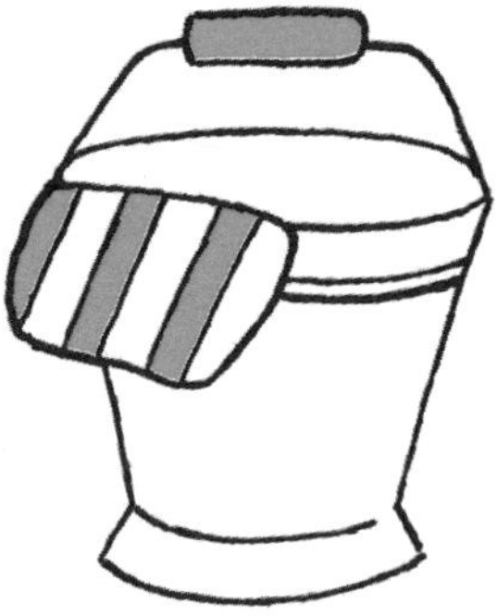

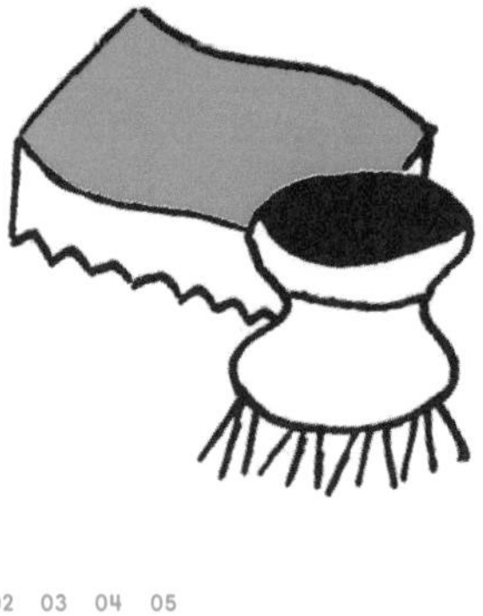

01 02 03 04 05

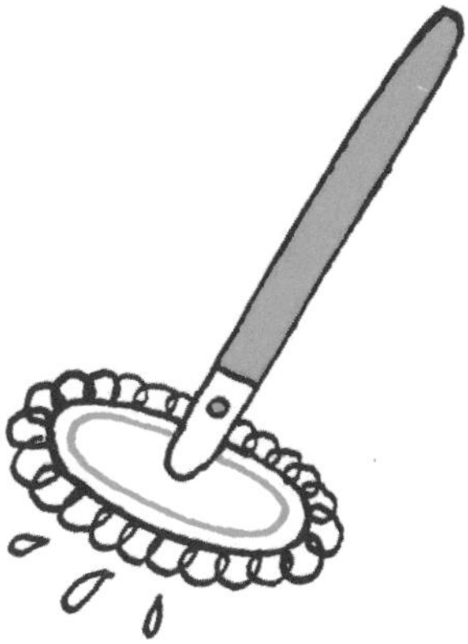

01 02 03 04 05

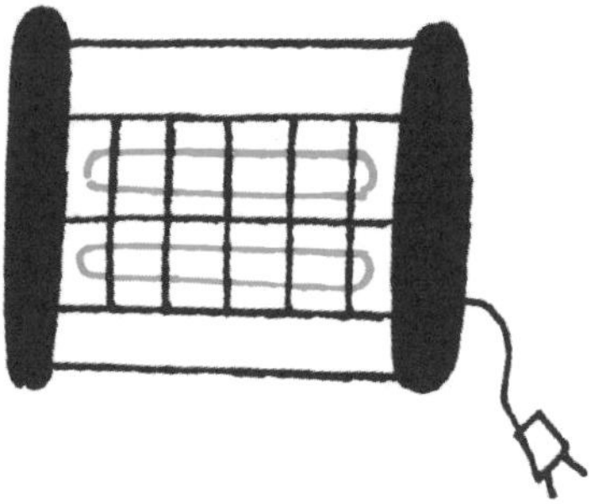

01 02 03 04 05

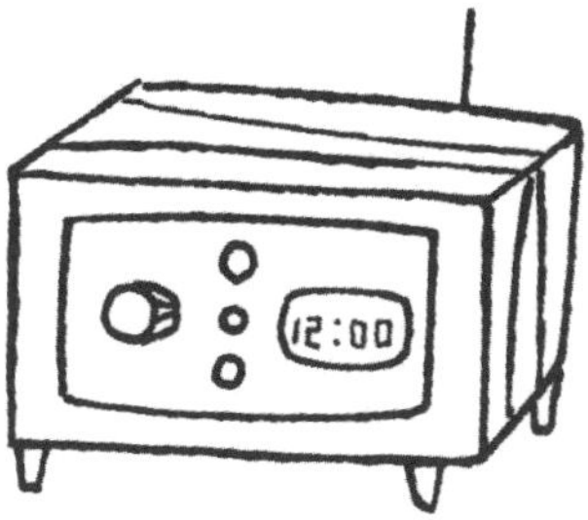

01 02 03 04 05

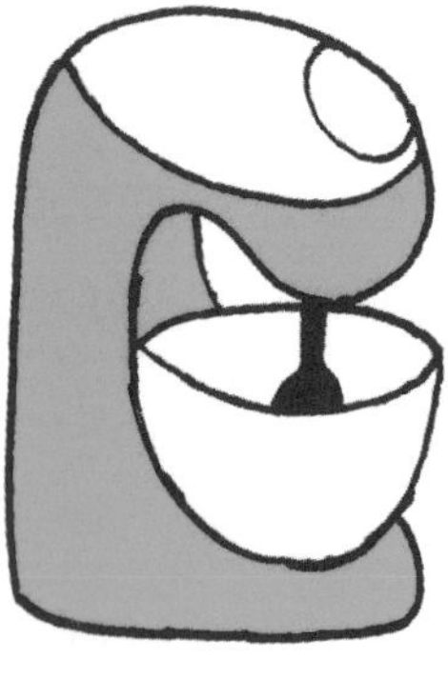

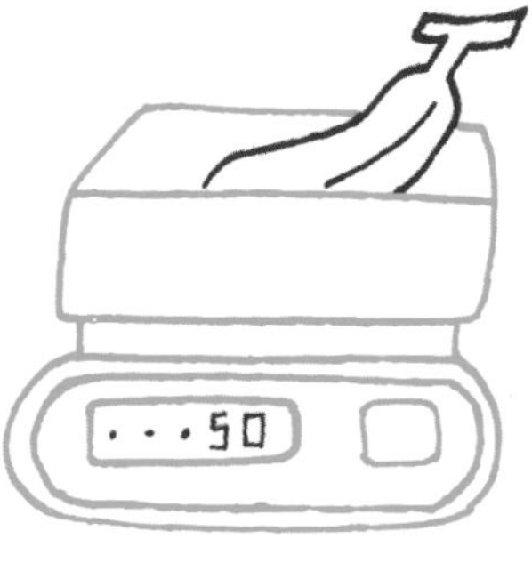

01 02 03 04 05

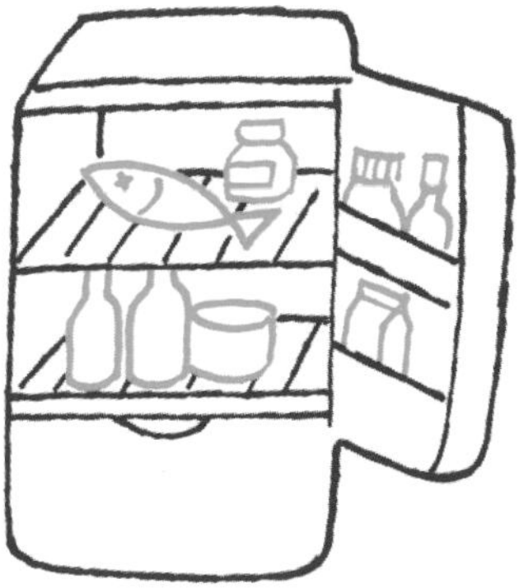

01 02 03 04 05

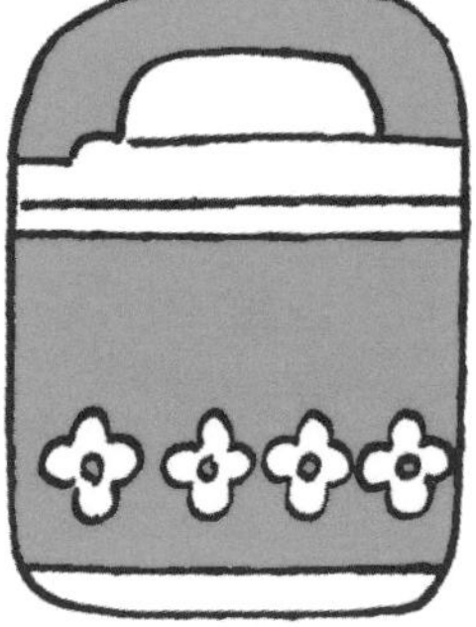

01 02 03 04

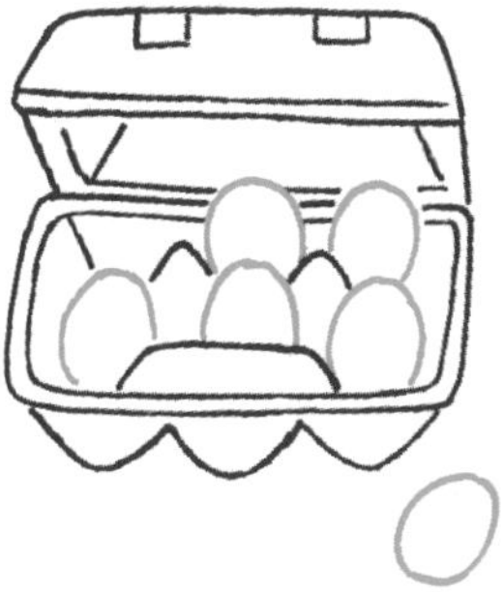

01 02 03 04 05

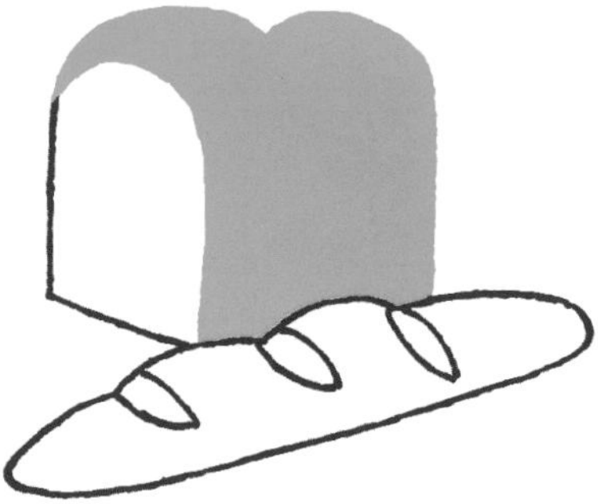

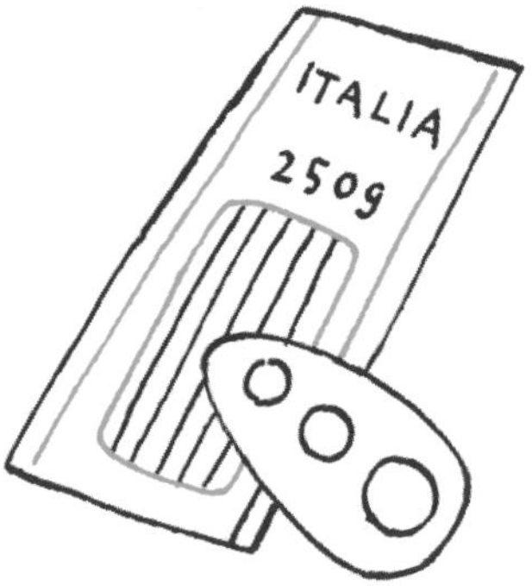

01 02 03 04

01 02 03 04 05

01 02 03 04

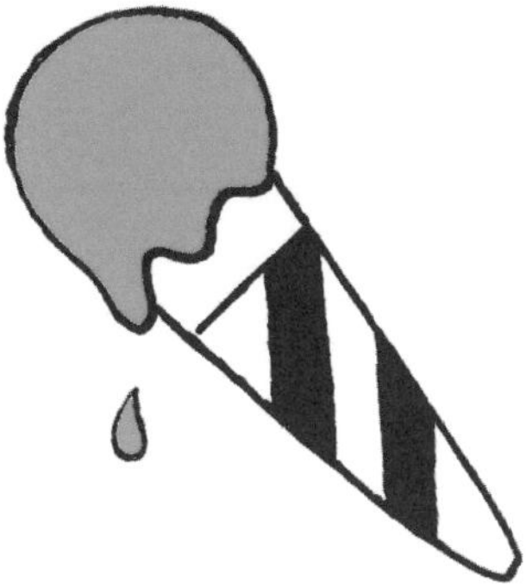

01 02 03 04 05

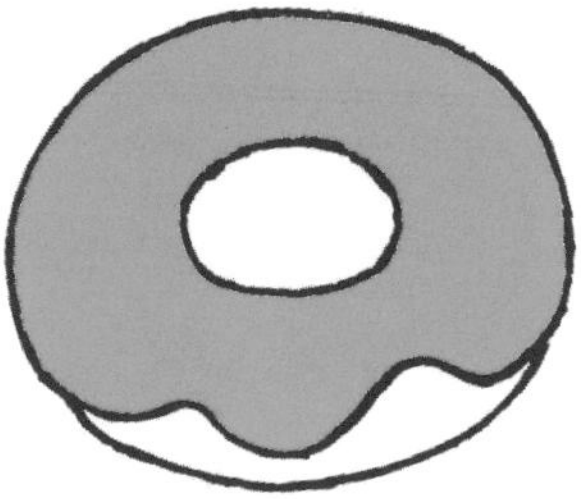

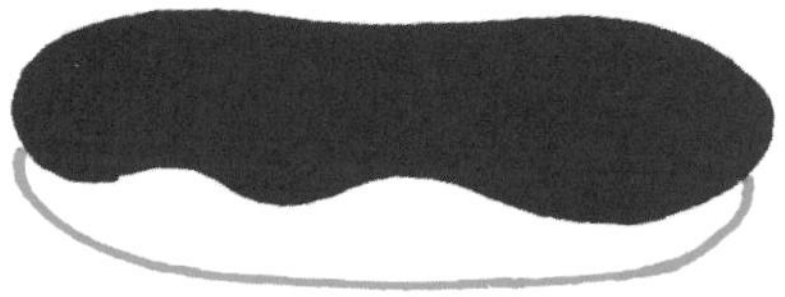

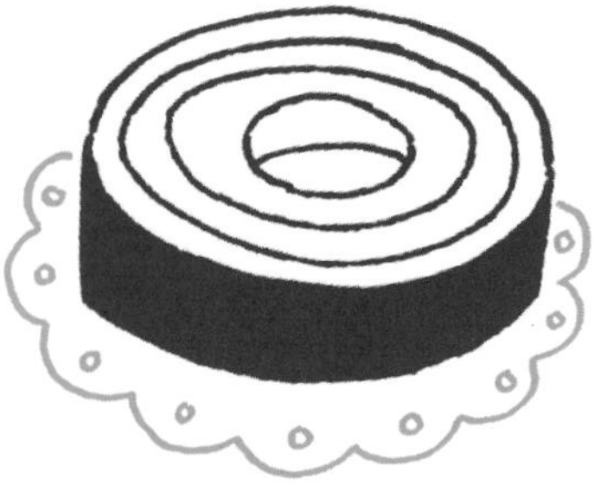

01 02 03 04 05

01 02 03 04

01 02 03 04 05

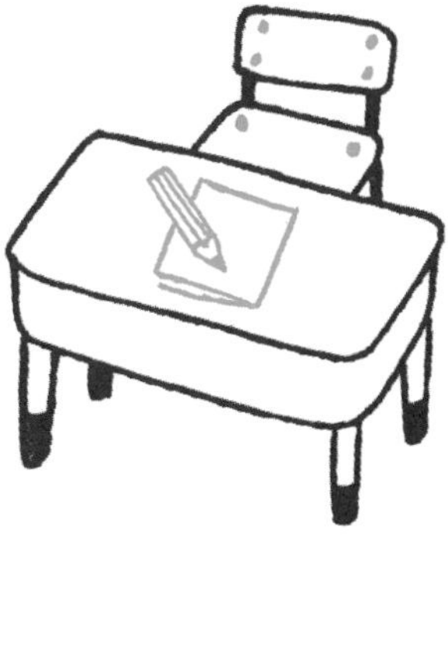

01 02 03 04 05

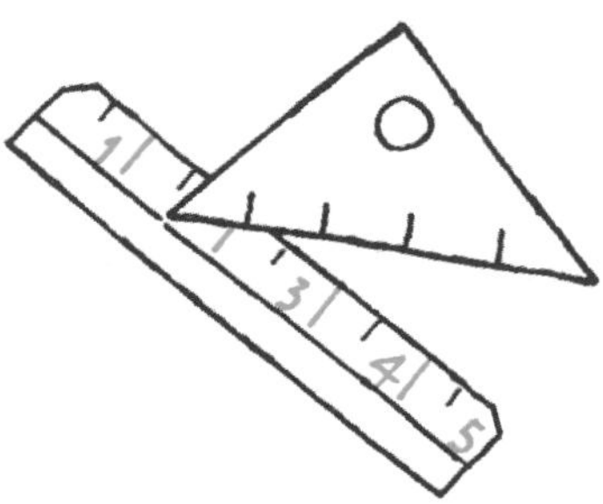

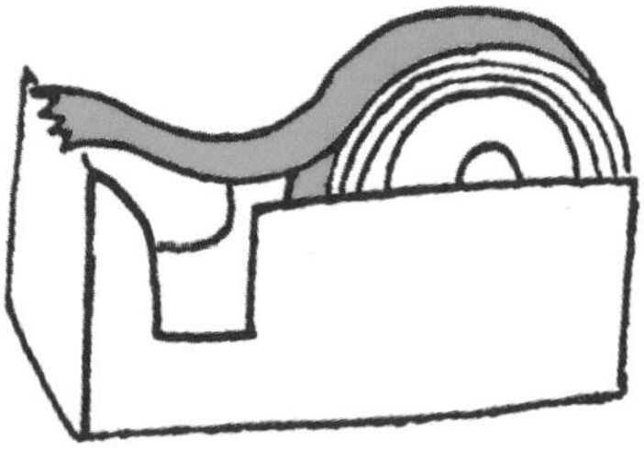

01 02 03 04 05

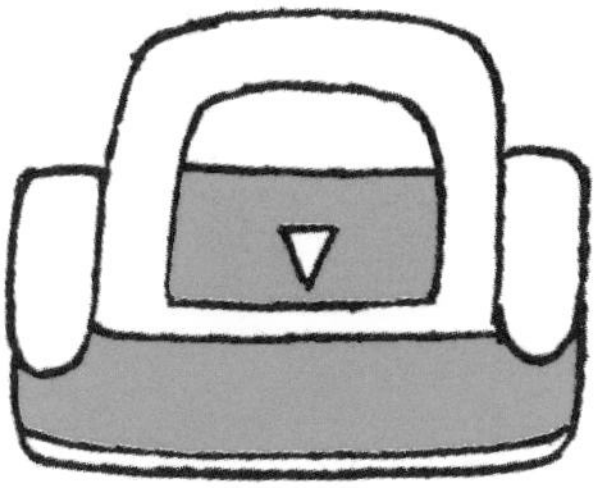

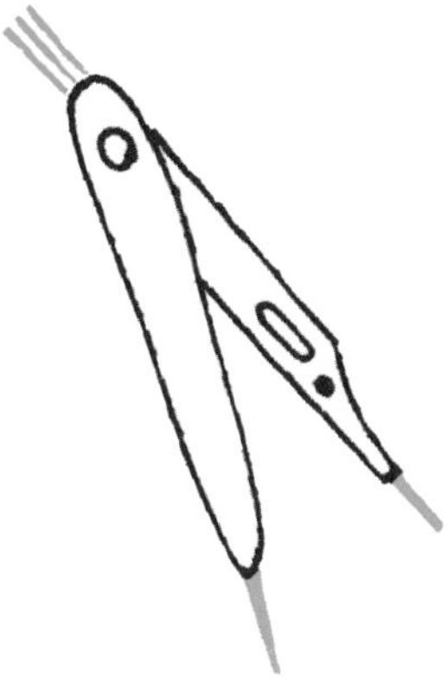

01 02 03 04 05

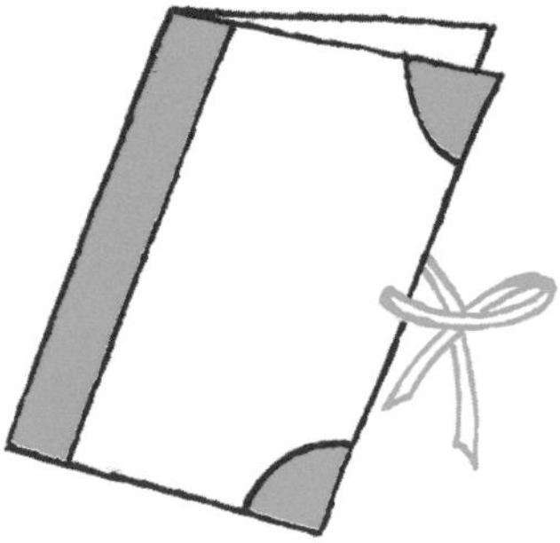

80

alubum

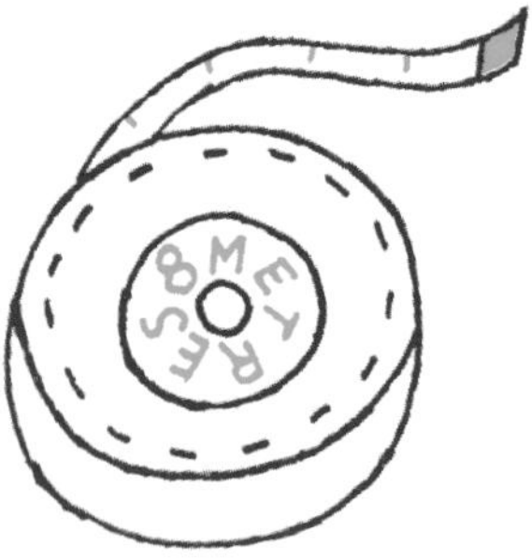
8 METRES

ink

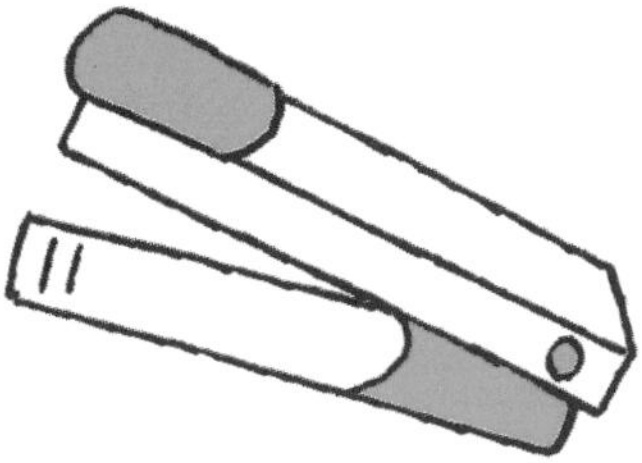

01 02 03 04 05

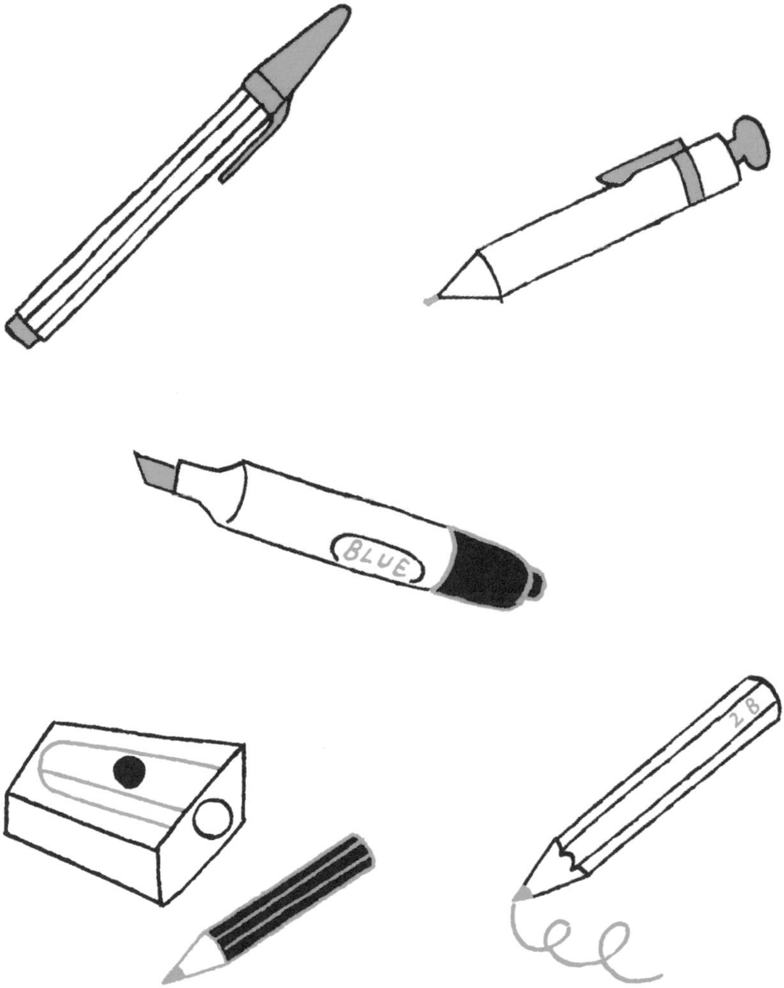

01 02 03 04 05

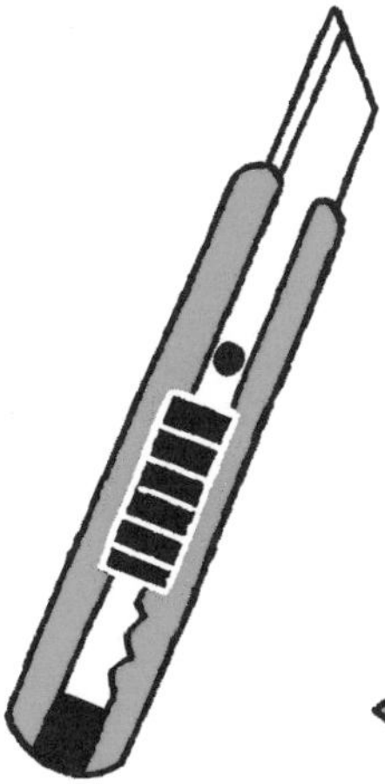

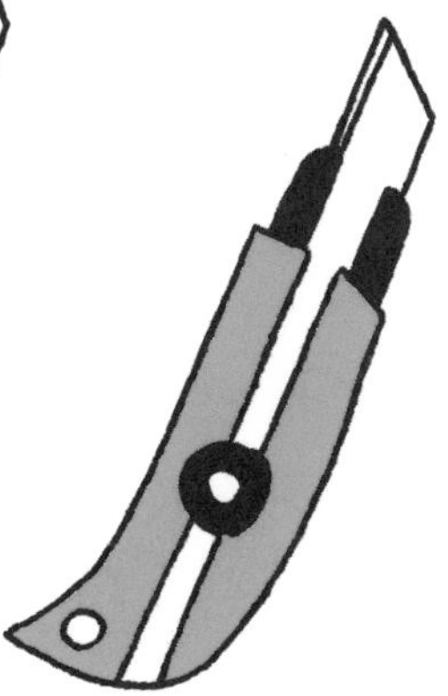

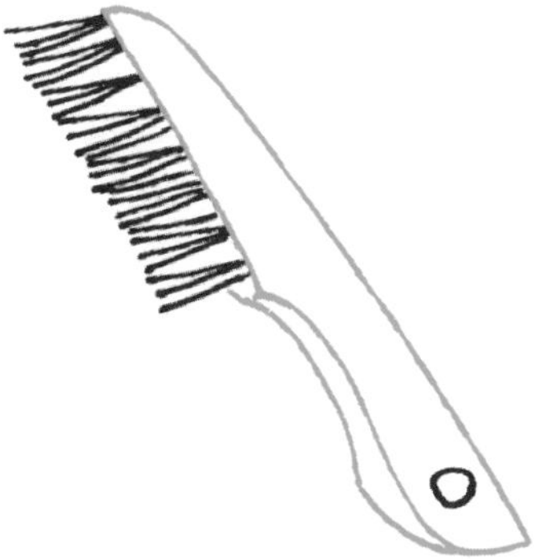

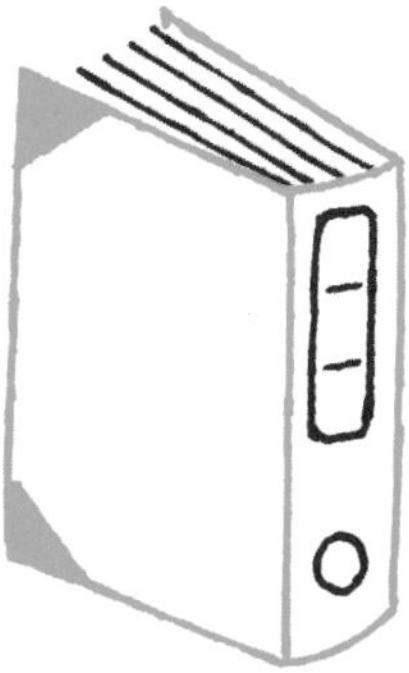

01 02 03 04 05

01 02 03 04 05

01 02 03 04 05

01 02 03 04 05

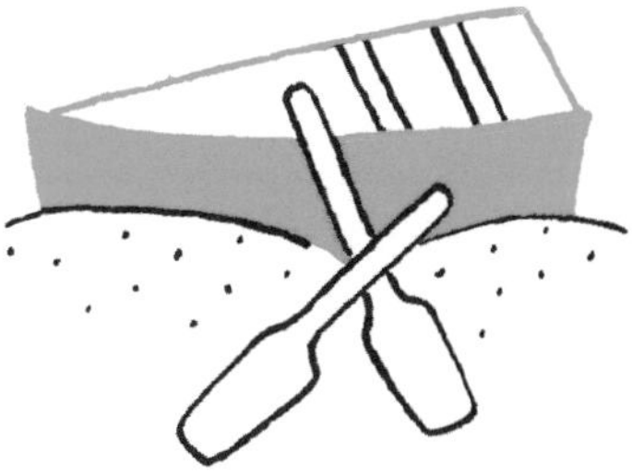

01 02 03 04 05

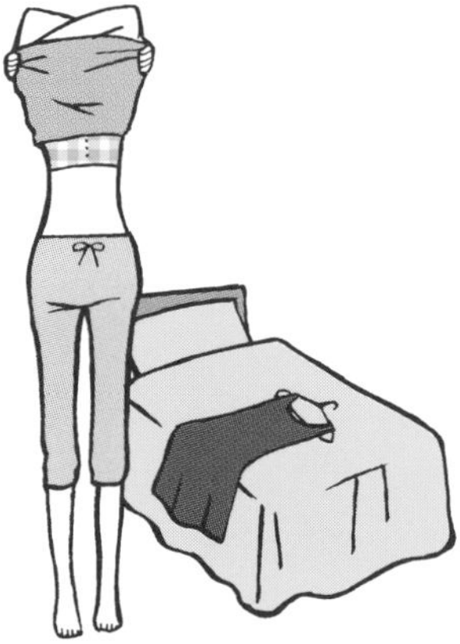

01 02 03 04 05 06

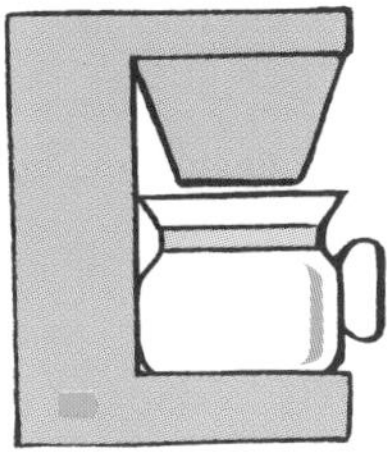

01 02 03 04 05

01 02 03 04 05

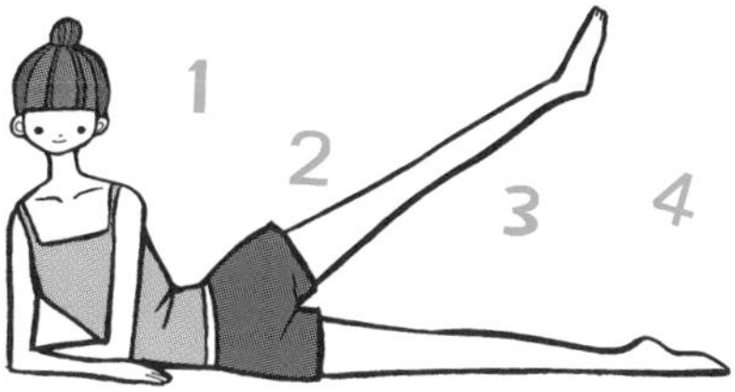

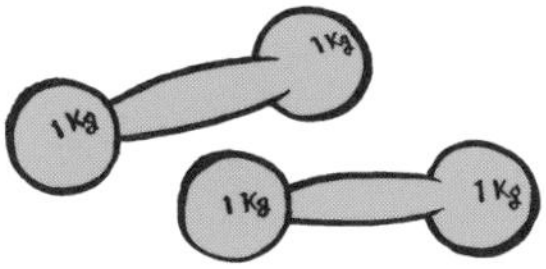

01 02 03 04 05

01

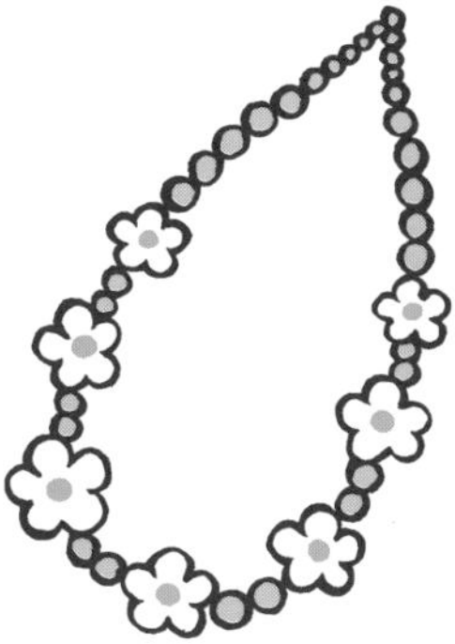

01 02 03 04 05 06 07

01 02 03 04 05 06 07

01 02 03 04 05 06

01 02 03 04 05 06 07

01 02 03 04 05 06 07

Candy
Candy

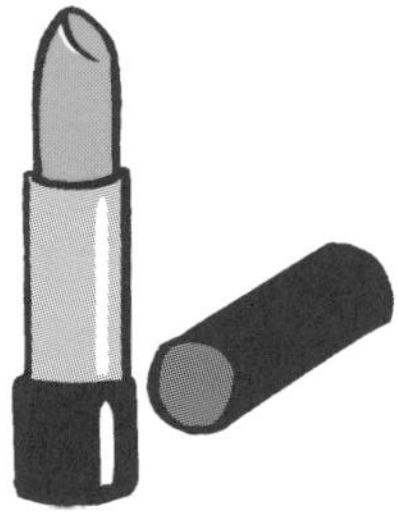

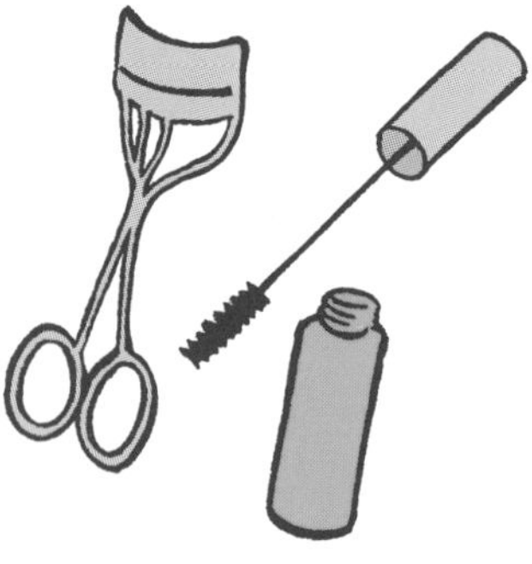

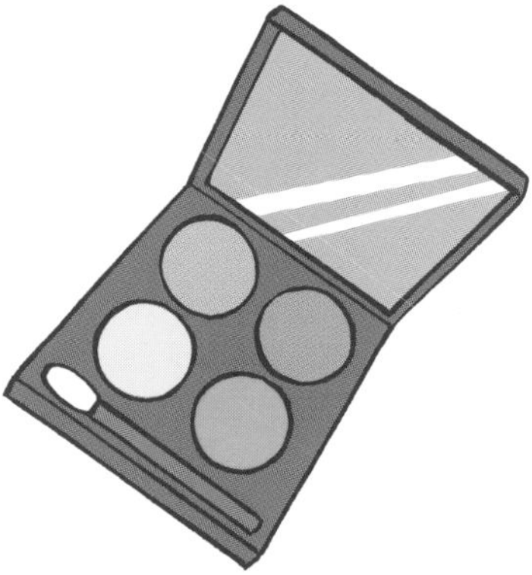

01 02 03 04 05

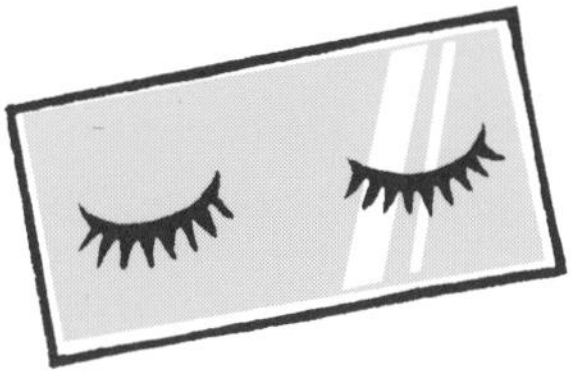

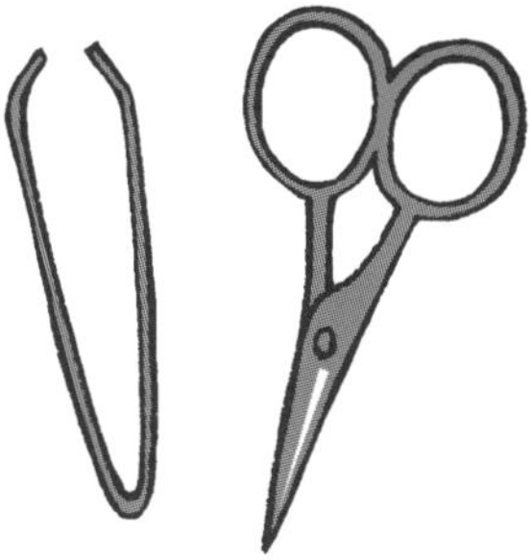

01 02 03 04 05

01 02 03 04 05

01 02 03 04 05

01 02 03 04

01 02

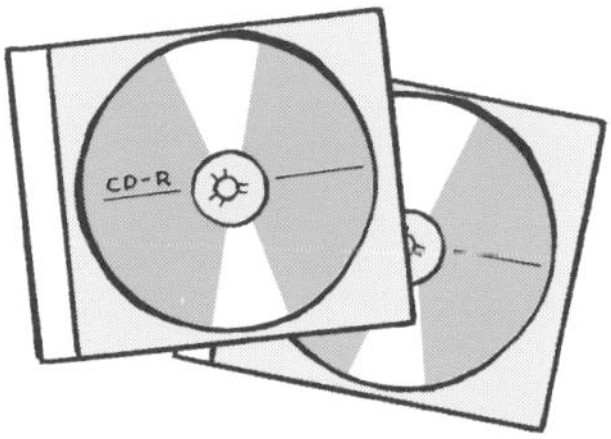

01 02 03 04 05

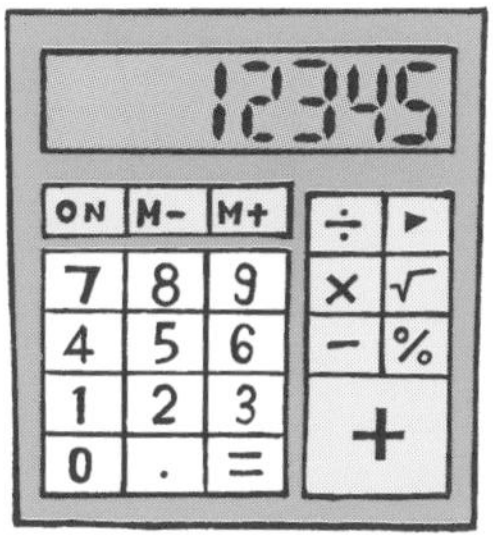
12345
ON M- M+ ÷ ▶
7 8 9 × √
4 5 6 − %
1 2 3 +
0 . =

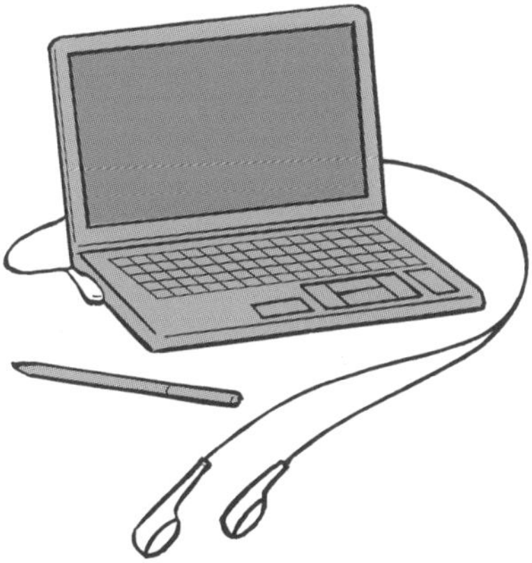

01 02 03 04

01 02 03 04 05

01 02 03 04 05

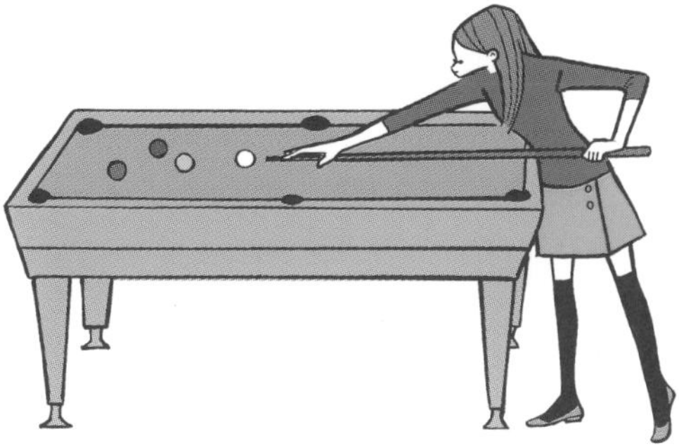

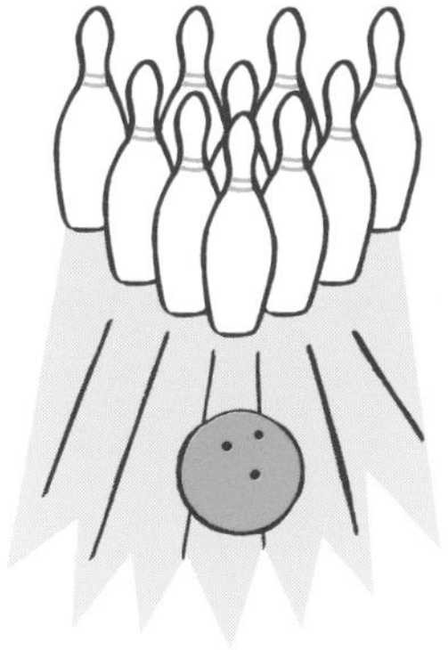

01 02 03 04 05

01 02 03 04 05

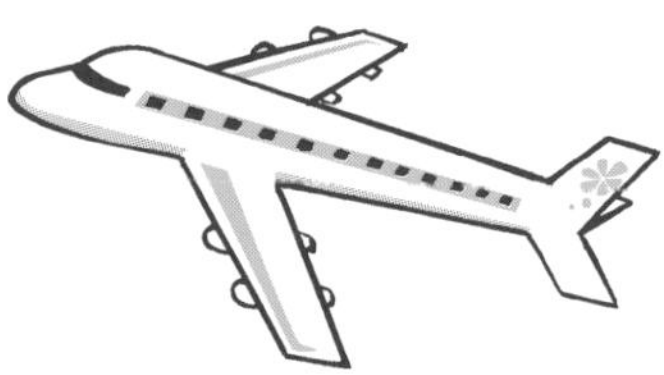

01 02 03 04 05

01 02 03 04 05

01 02 03 04 05

01 02 03 04 05

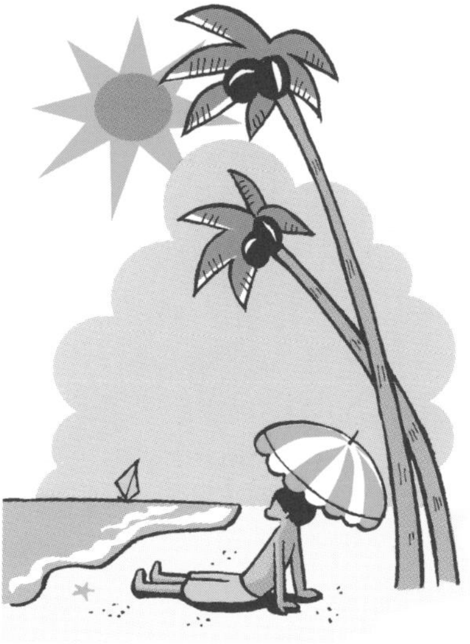

01 02 03 04

01 02 03 04 05

01 02 03 04 05

01 02 03 04

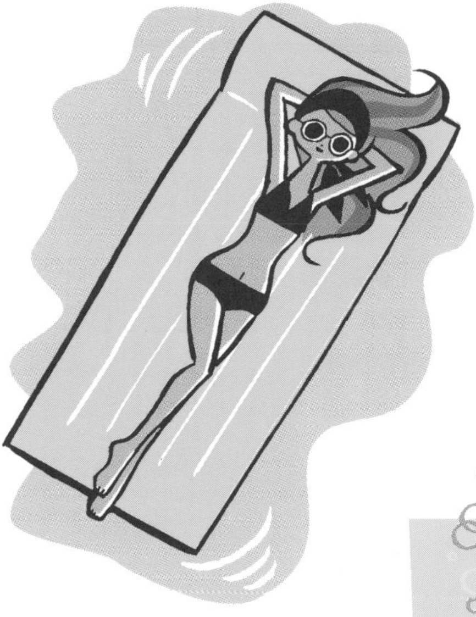

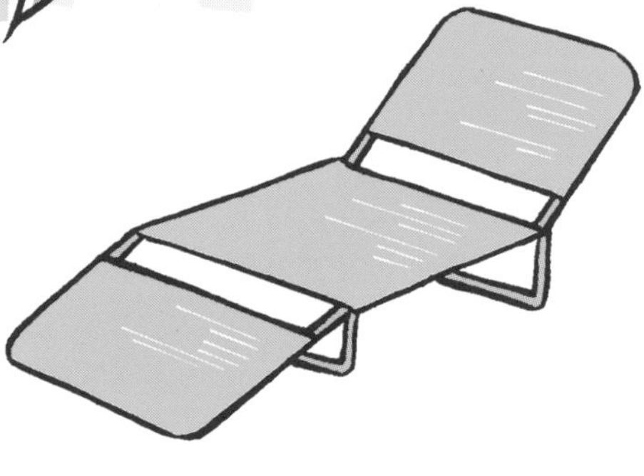

01 02 03 04 05

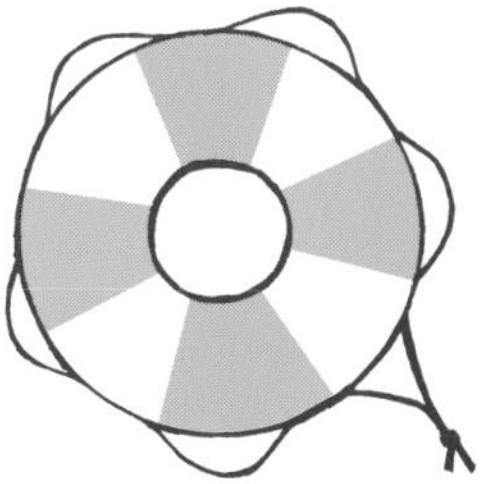

01 02 03 04 05

01 02 03 04

01

01 02 03 04

01 02 03 04

01 02 03 04 05

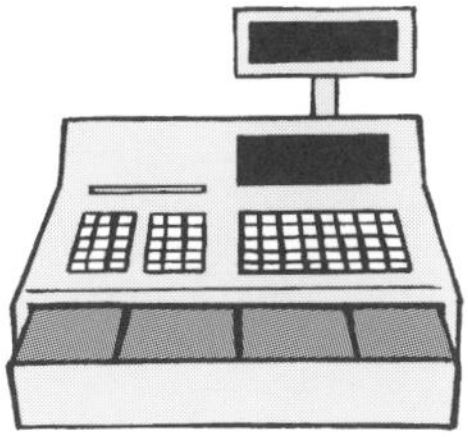

01 02 03 04 05

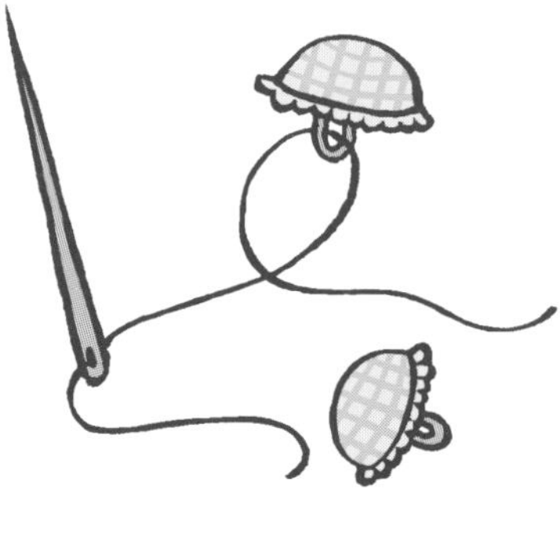

01 02 03 04 05

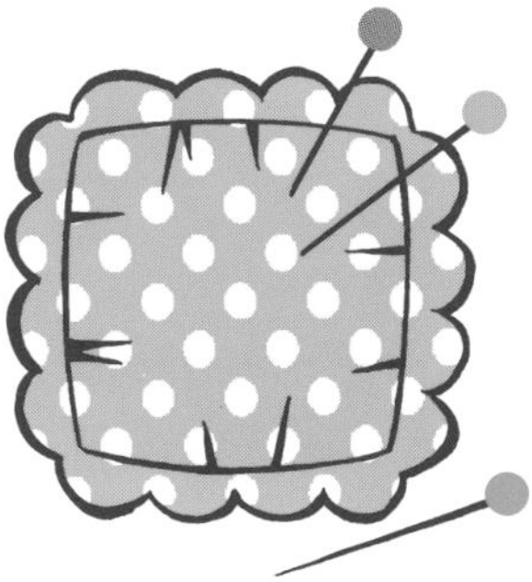

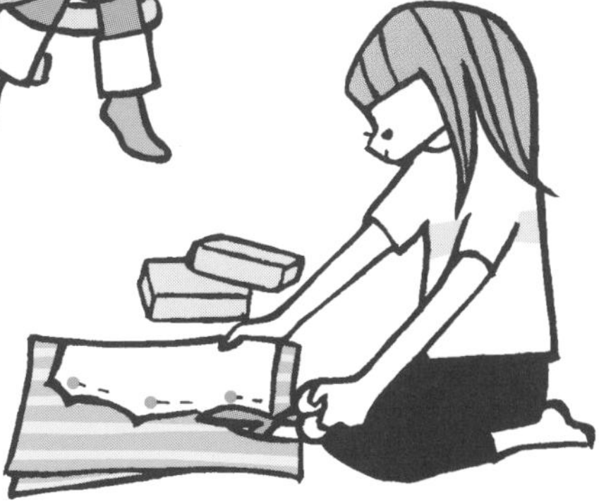

01 02 03 04 05

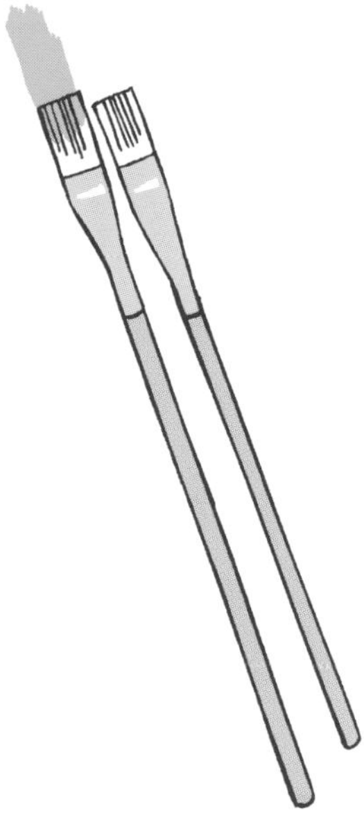

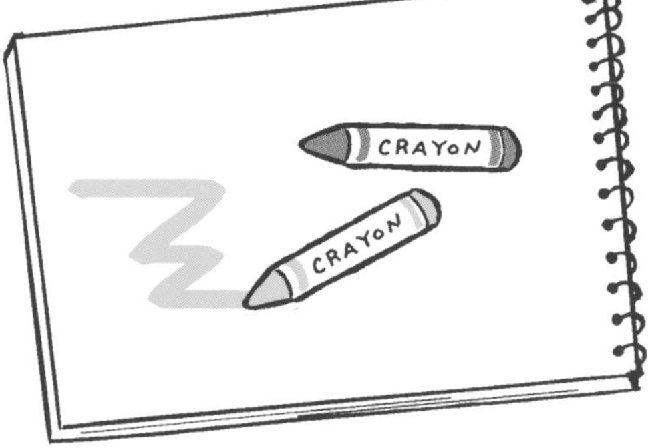

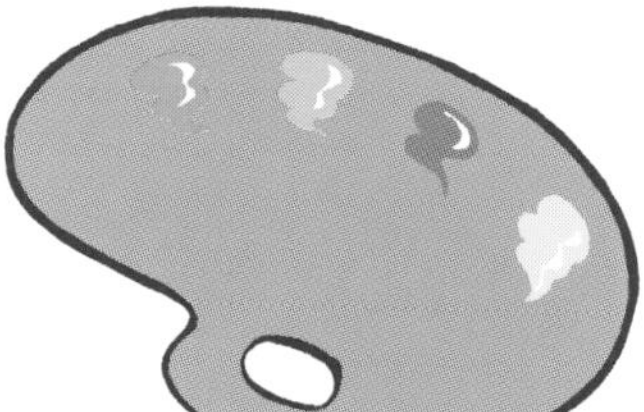

01 02 03 04 05

01 02 03 04 05

01 02 03 04 05

01 02 03

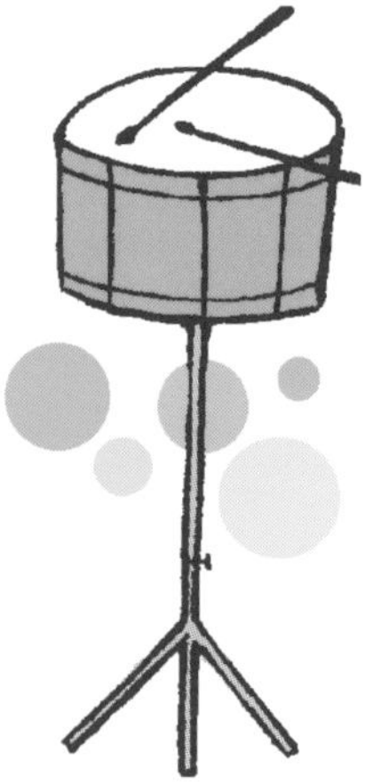

01 02 03 04

01 02 03 04

01 02 03 04

01 02 03 04

01 02 03 04 05

01 02 03 04 05

01 02 03

01 02 03 04 05

01 02 03 04 05

01 02 03 04 05

01 02 03 04 05

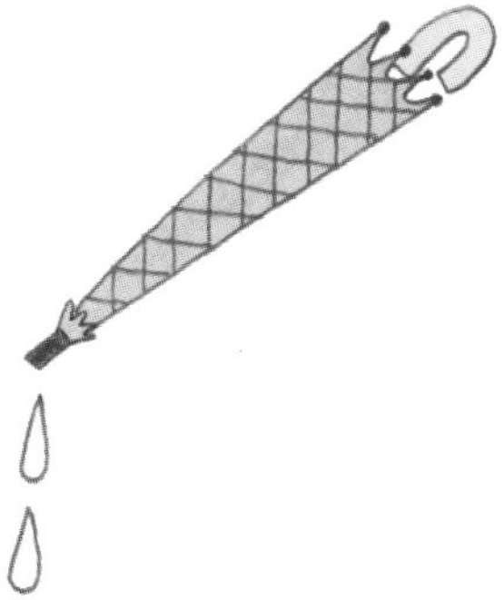

01 02 03 04 05

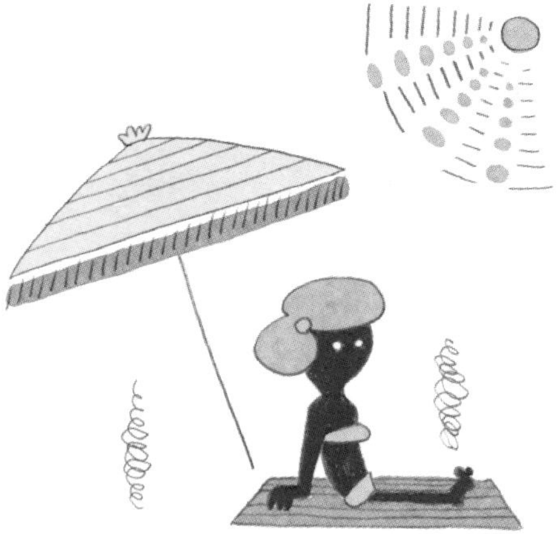

01 02 03

01 02

01 02 03 04 05

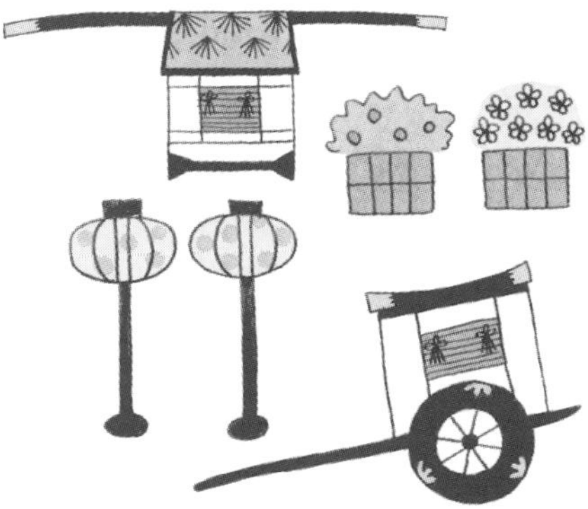

Happy
Mother's Day!

You're
my hero, Dad!

Happy
Father's Day!

01 02 03 04

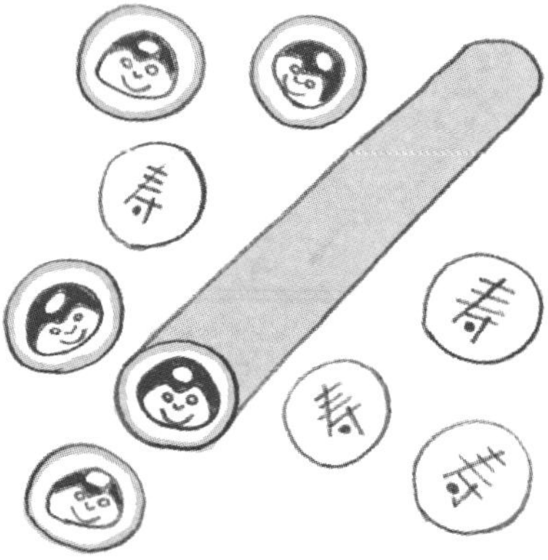

01 02 03

01 02 03 04 05

01 02 03 04 05

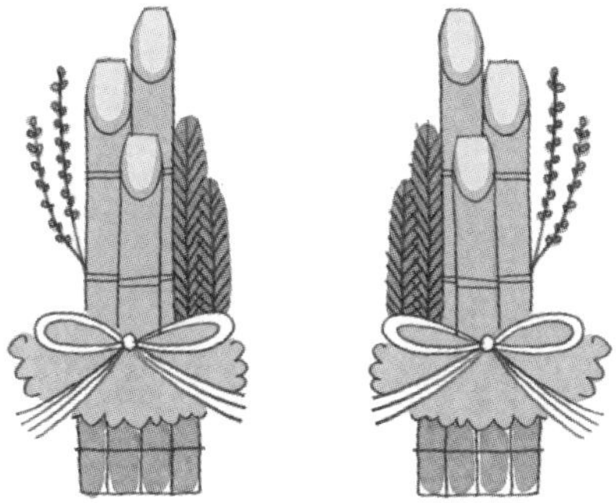

01 02 03 04 05

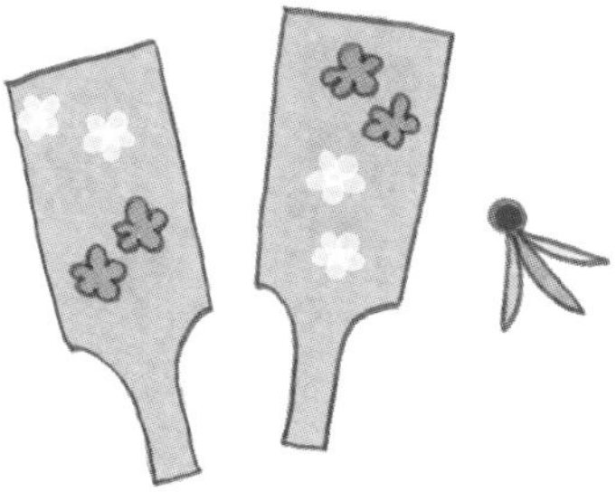

01 02 03 04 05

01 02 03 04 05

01 02 03 04

01 02 03 04

01 02 03 04

01 02 03 04

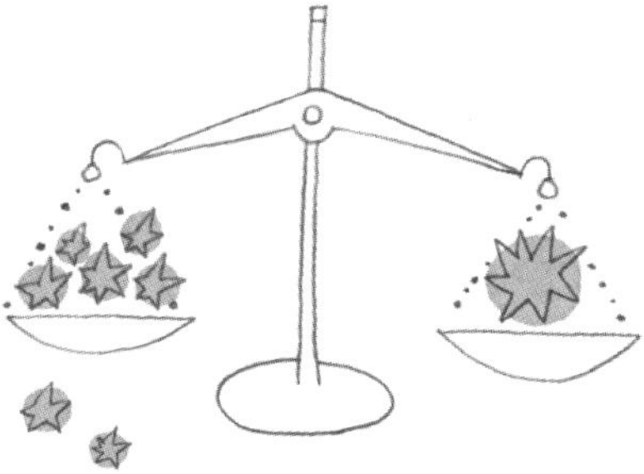

01 02 03 04

01 02 03 04

01 02 03 04

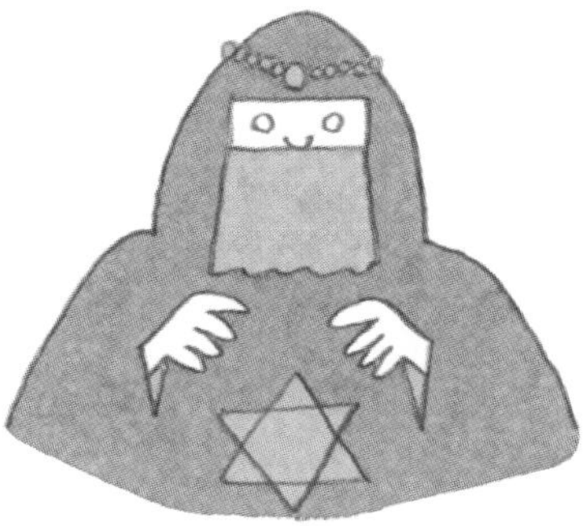

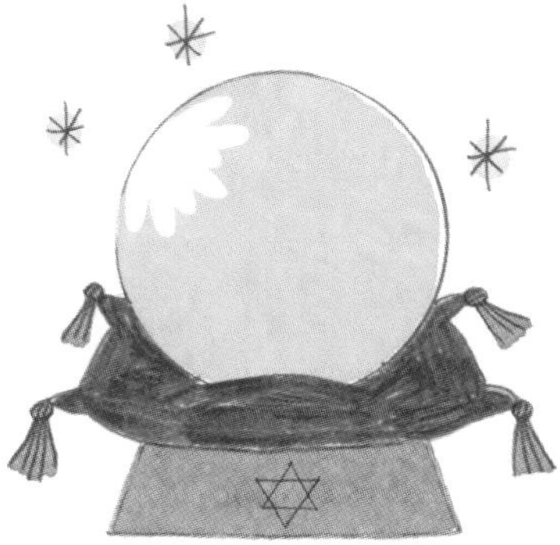

01 02

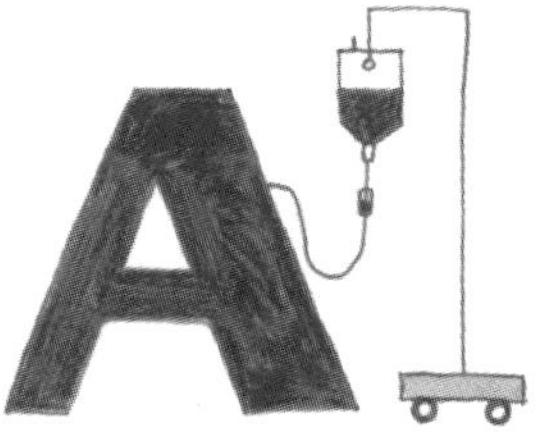

Blood Type A

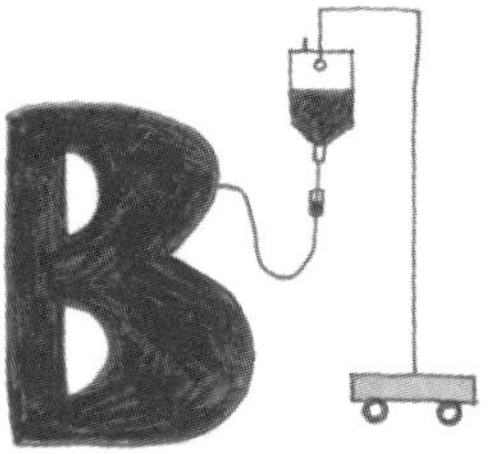

Blood Type B

Blood Type AB

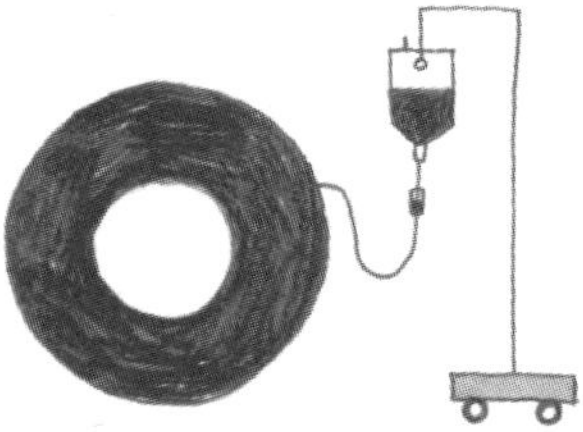

Blood Type O

01 02 03 04

01 02 03 04 05

BIRTHDAY PARTY

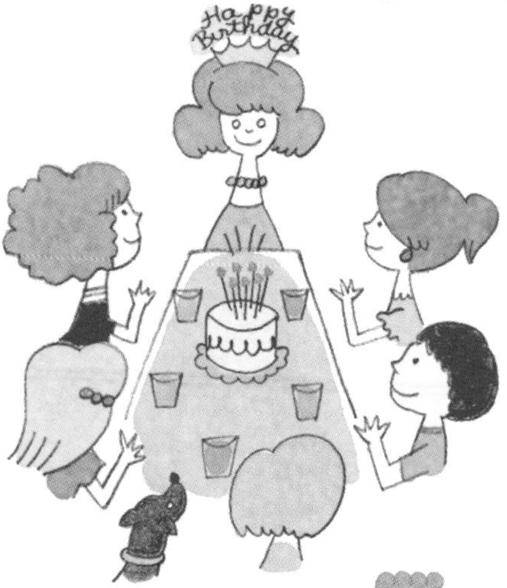

Happy Birthday

Happy Birthday

HAPPY BIRTHDAY

01 02 03 04 05

01 02 03 04 05

01 02 03 04 05

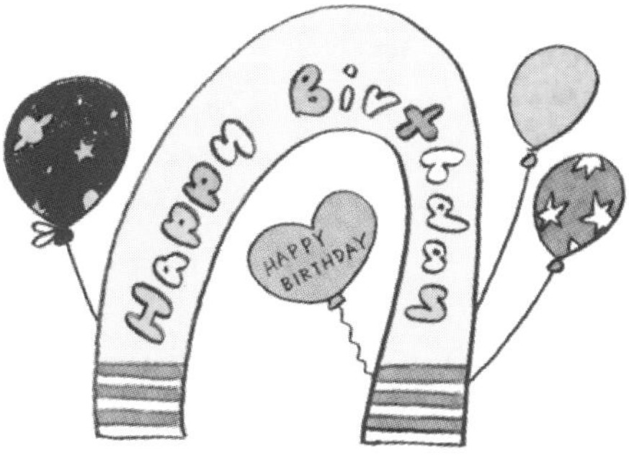

01 02 03

01 02 03 04

01 02 03 04 05

01 02 03 04 05 06

01 02 03 04 05

01 02 03 04 05

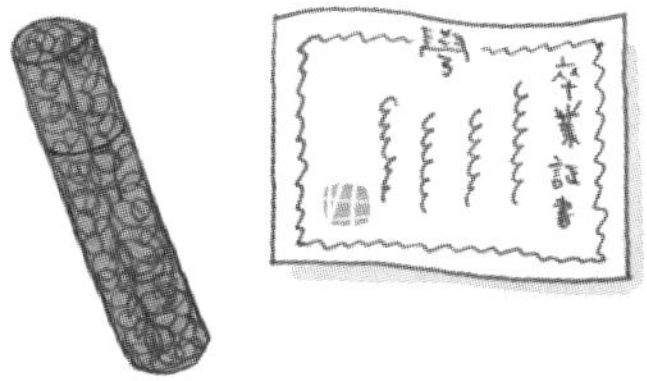

01 02 03 04 05 06

01 02 03 04 05

Welcome
to
our
Wedding
Party

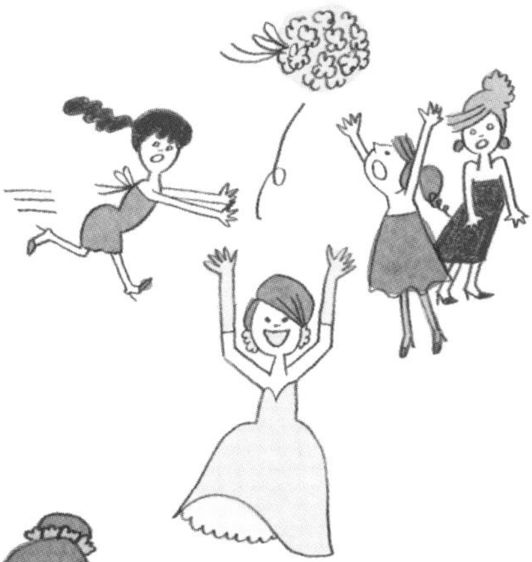

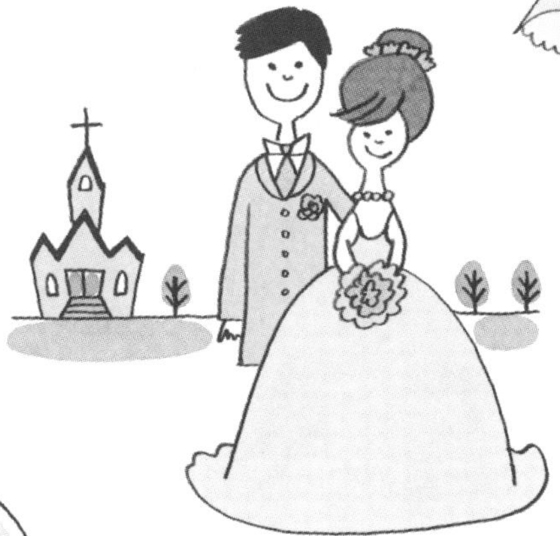

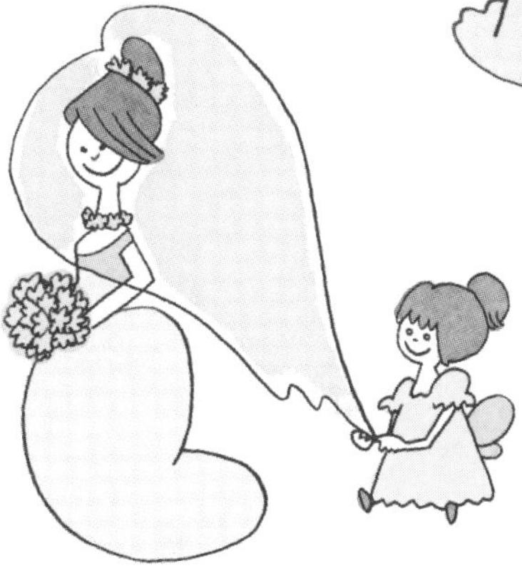

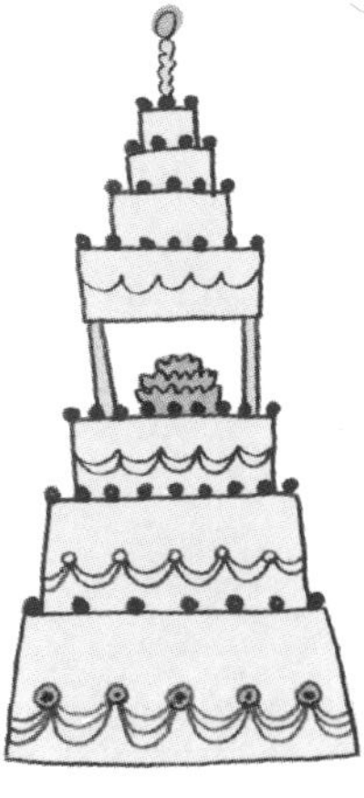

01 02 03 04 05

01

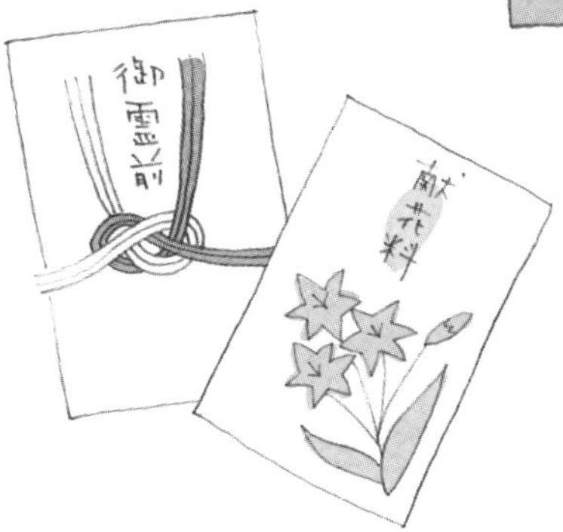

01 02 03 04 05

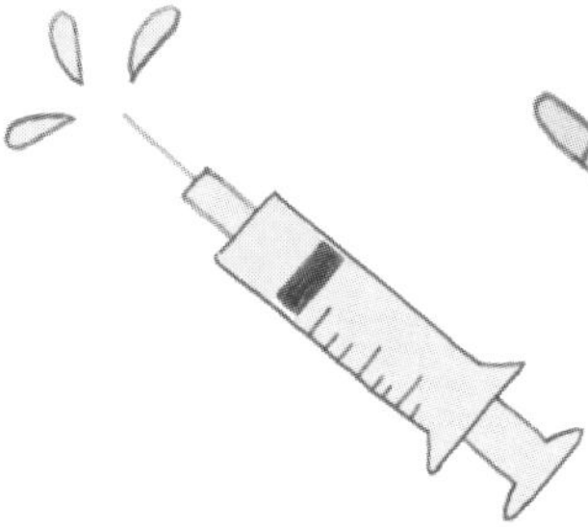

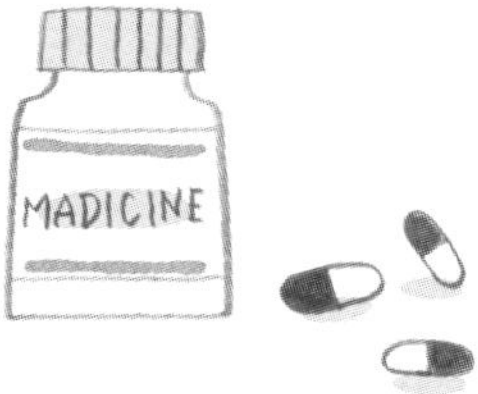

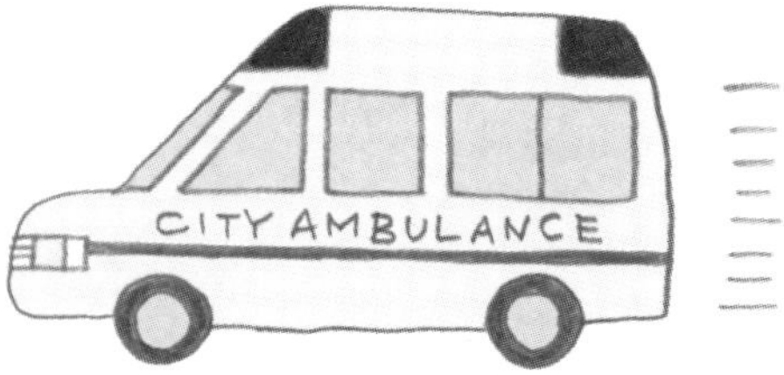

01 02 03 04 05 06 07

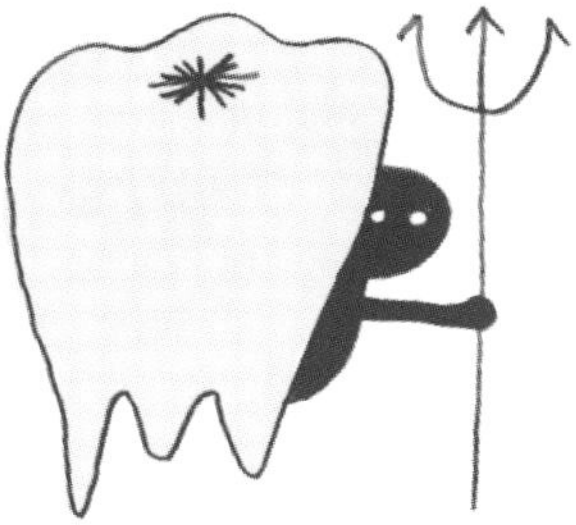

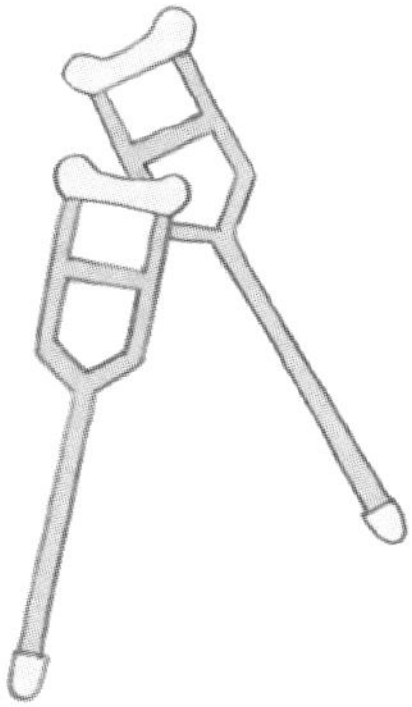

01 02 03 04 05

01 02 03 04 05

01 02 03 04 05

01 02 03 04 05

01 02 03 04 05

01 02 03 04 05

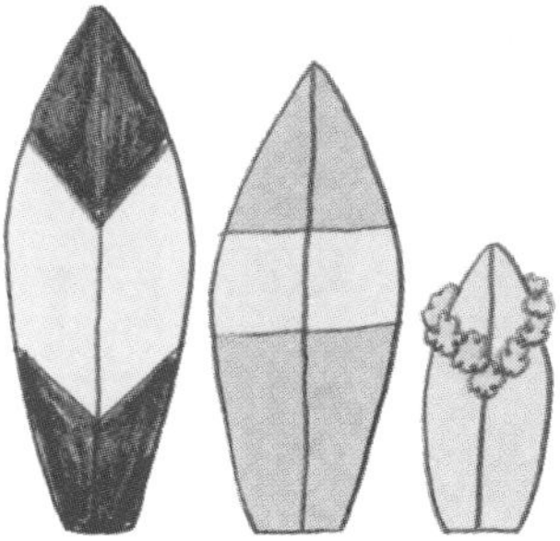

01 02 03 04 05

01 02 03 04 05

01 02 03 04 05

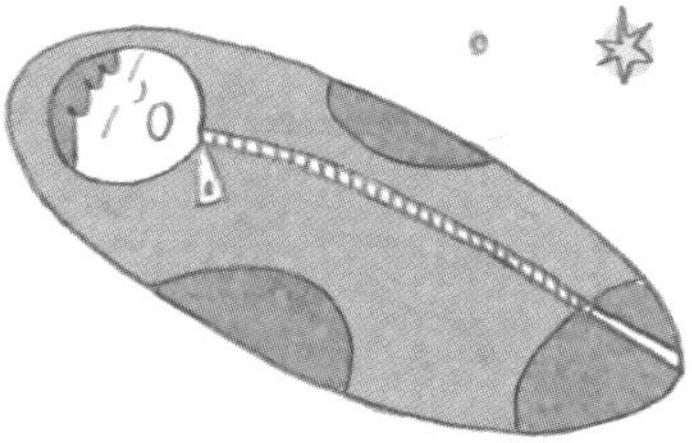

01 02 03 04 05 06

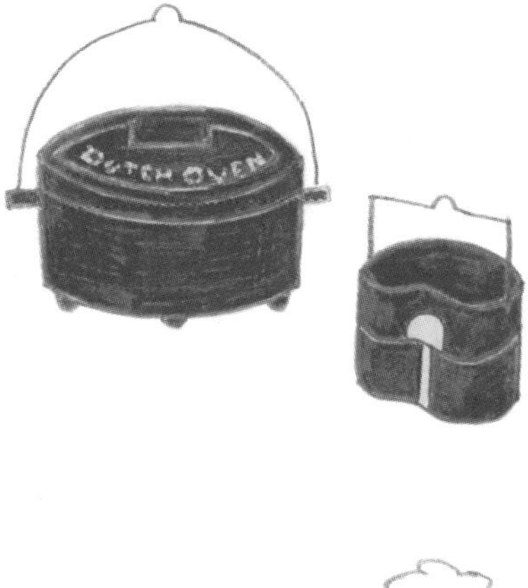

01 02 03 04 05 06

01 02 03 04 05

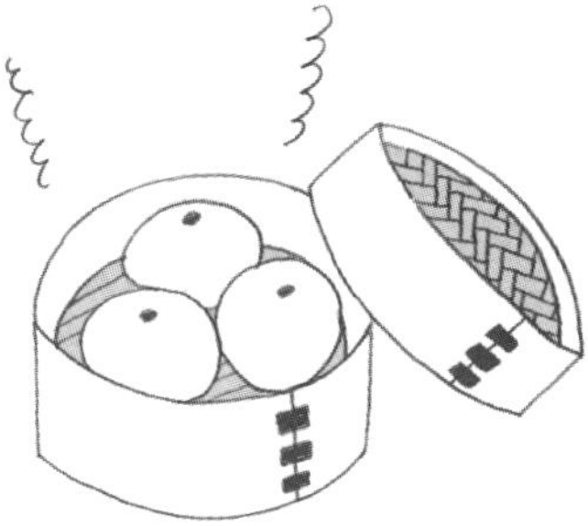

01 02 03 04

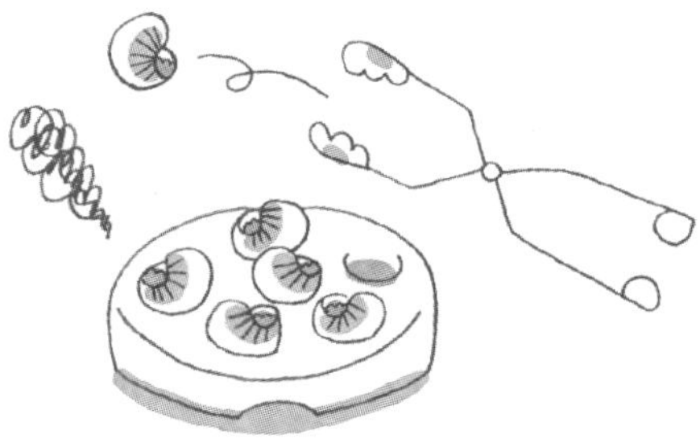

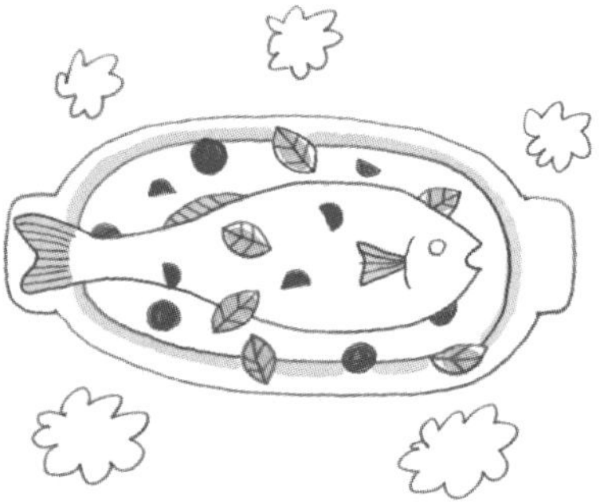

01 02 03 04 05

01 02 03 04 05

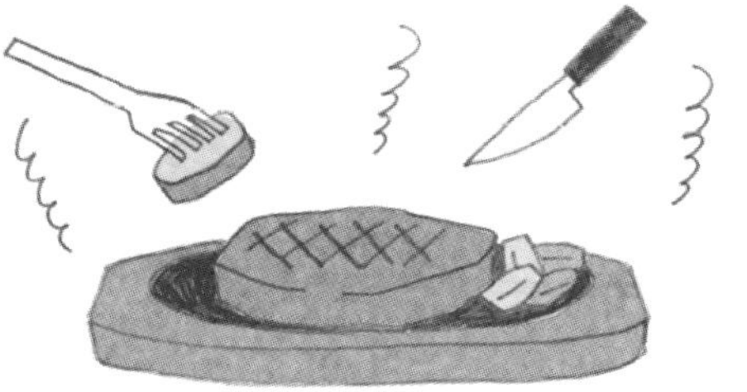

01 02 03 04 05

01 02 03 04 05

01　02　03　04

01 02 03

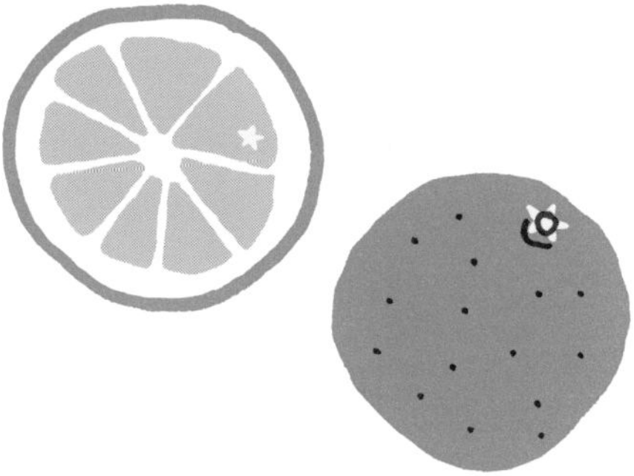

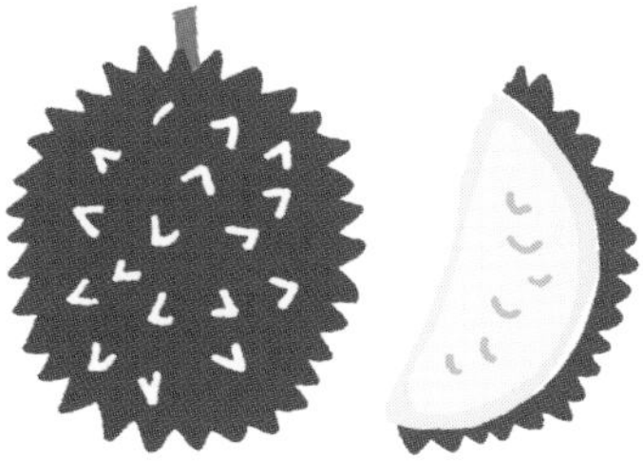

01 02 03 04 05

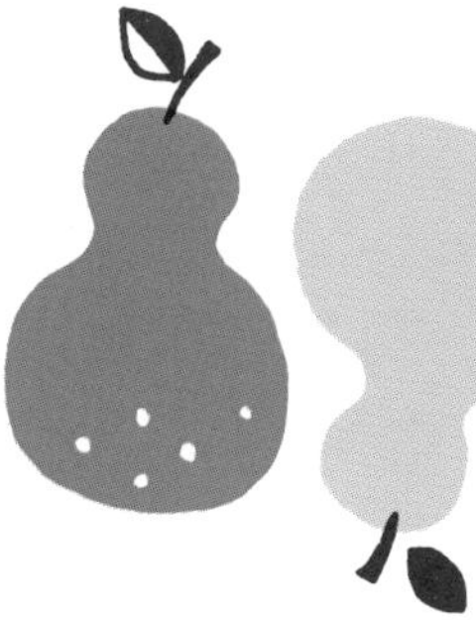

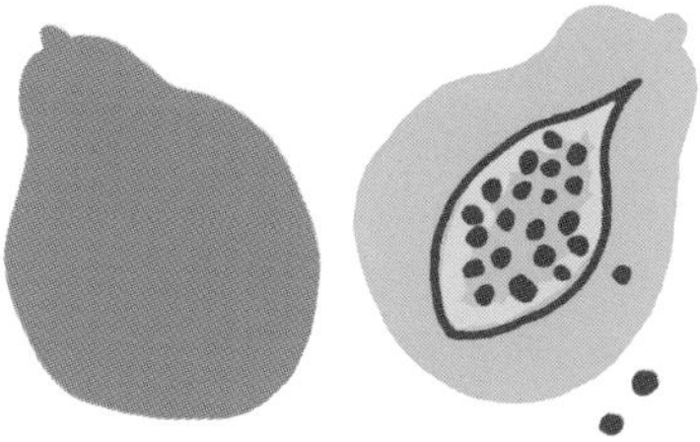

01 02 03 04 05

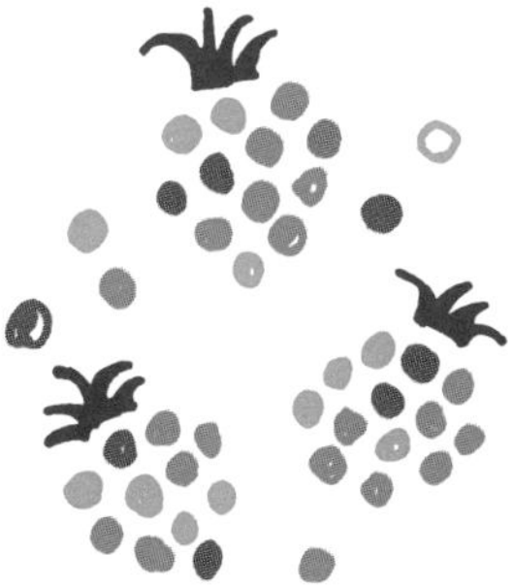

01 02 03 04 05

01 02 03 04 05 06

01 02 03 04 05

01 02 03 04 05

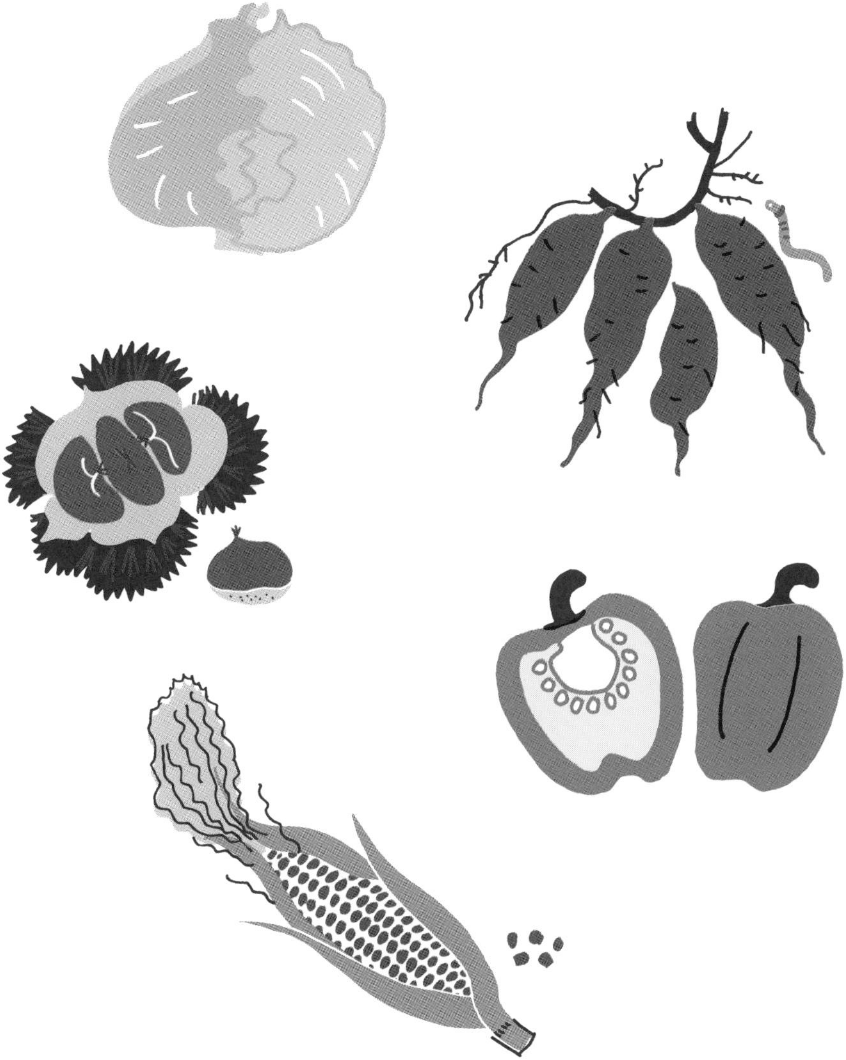

01 02 03 04 05

01 02 03 04 05

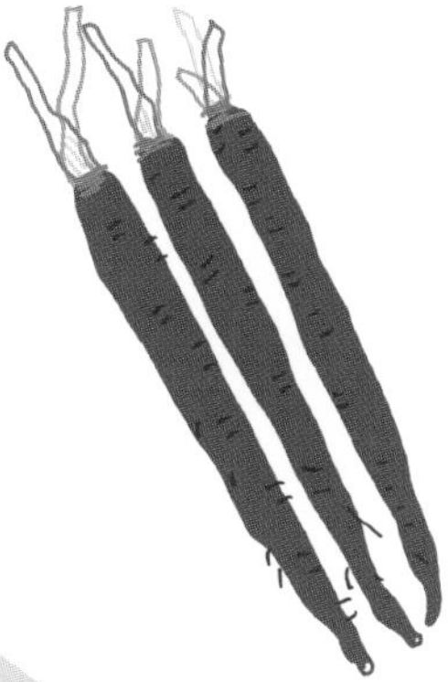

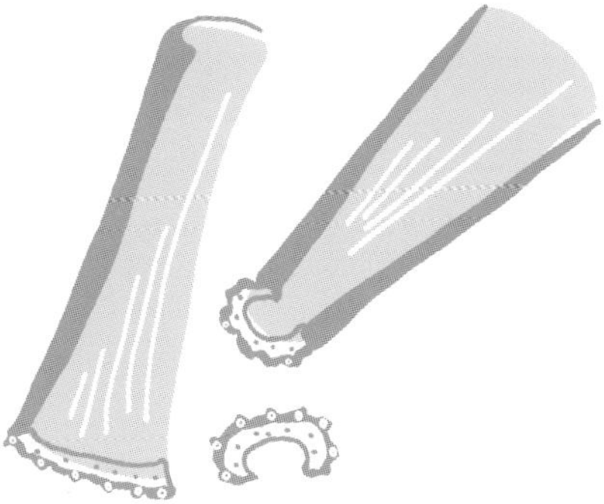

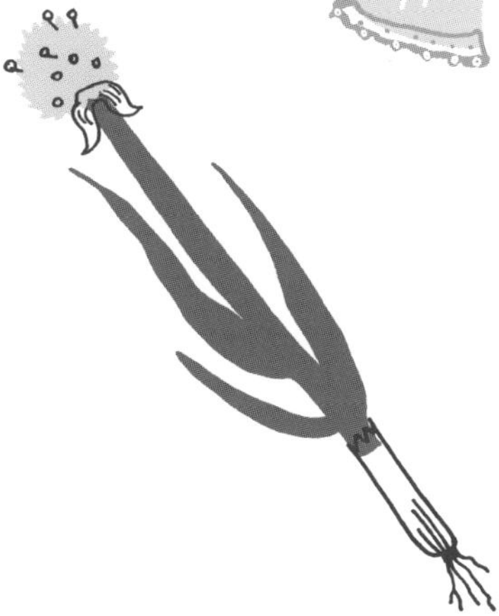

01 02 03 04 05

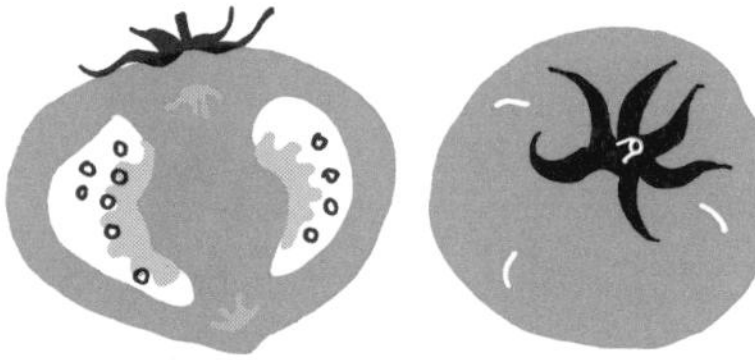

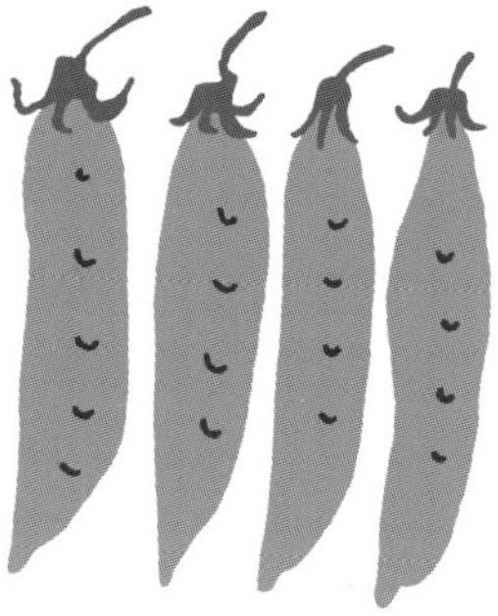

01 02 03 04

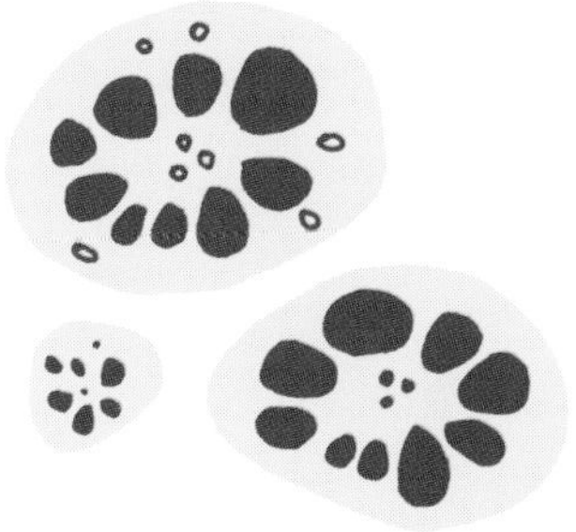

01 02 03 04 05

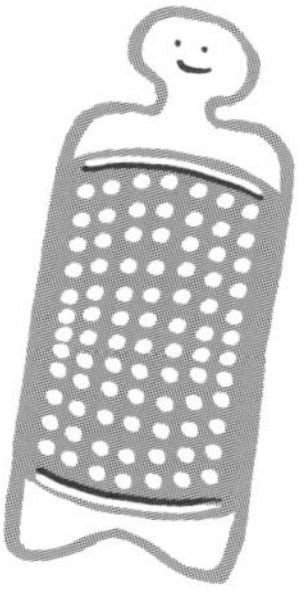

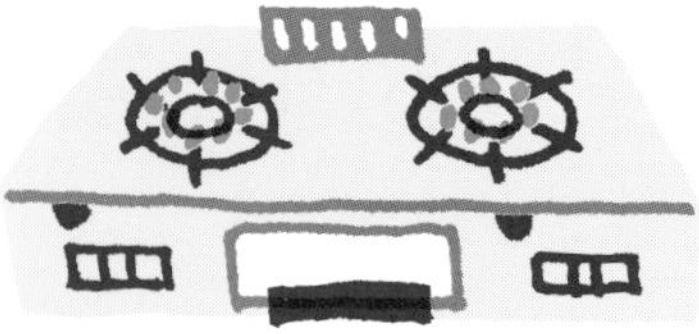

01 02 03 04 05 06

01 02 03 04

01 02 03 04 05 06

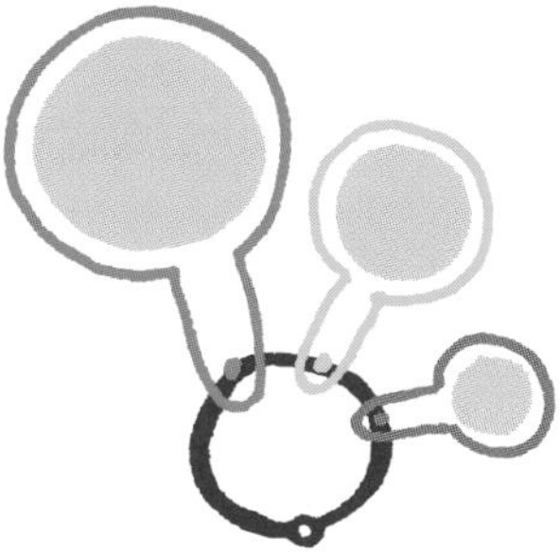

01 02 03 04 05

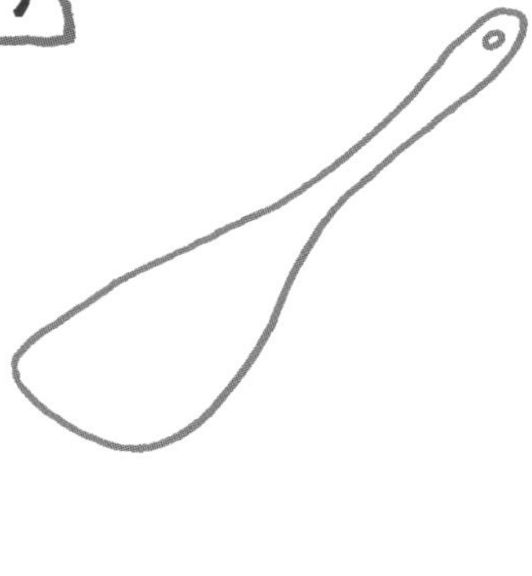

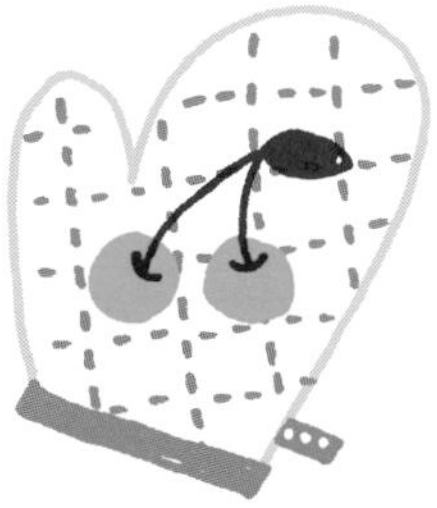

01 02 03 04 05

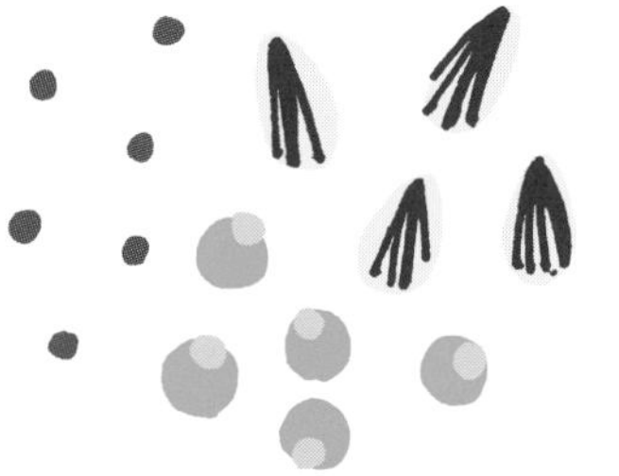

01 02 03 04 05

01 02 03 04 05

01 02 03 04 05

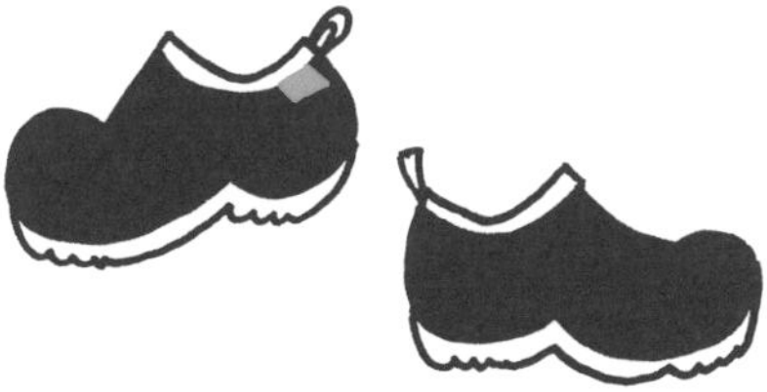

01 02 03 04 05

01 02 03 04

01

01 02 03 04 05

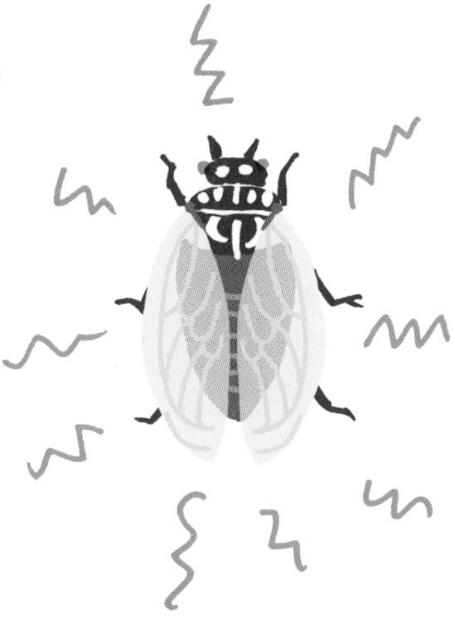

01 02 03 04 05

01 02 03 04

01 02 03 04

01 02 03 04 05

01 02 03 04 05

01 02 03

01 02 03

01 02 03 04 05

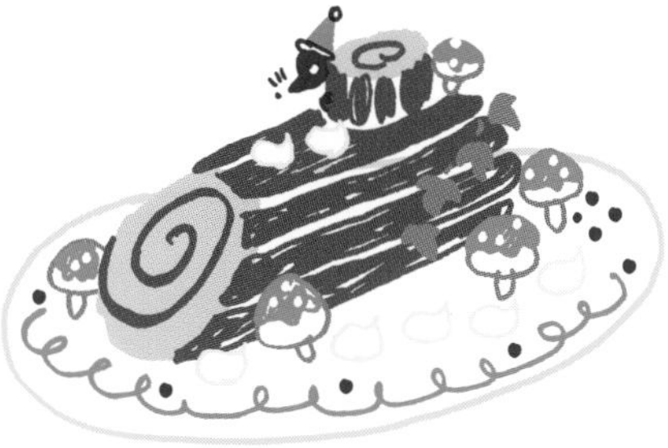

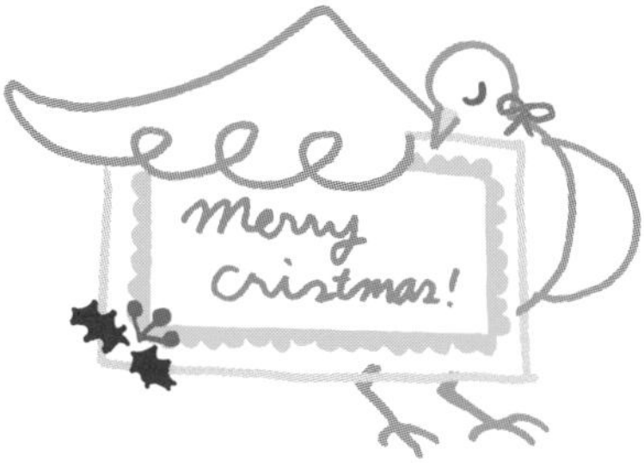
Merry
Cristmas!

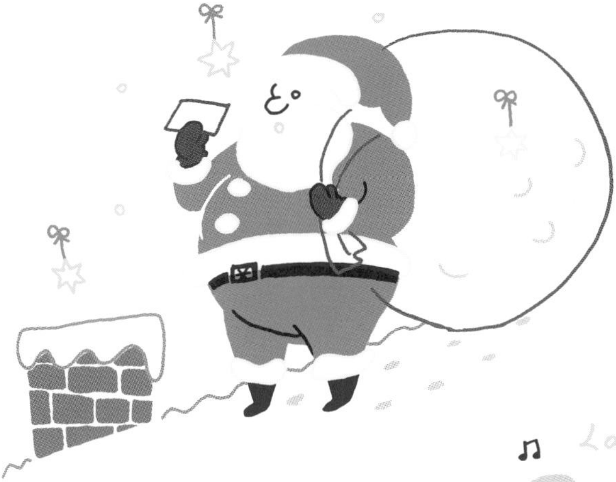

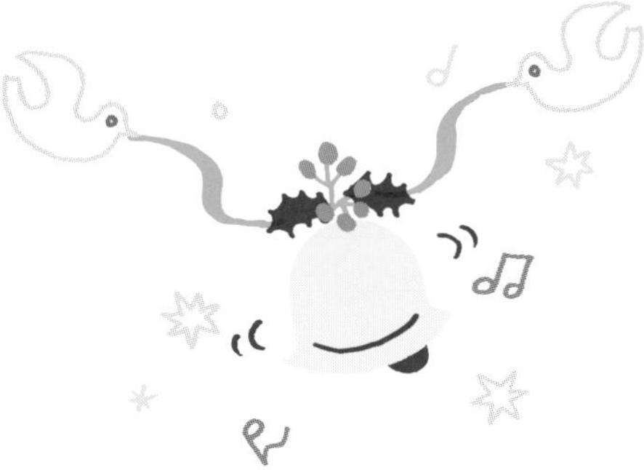

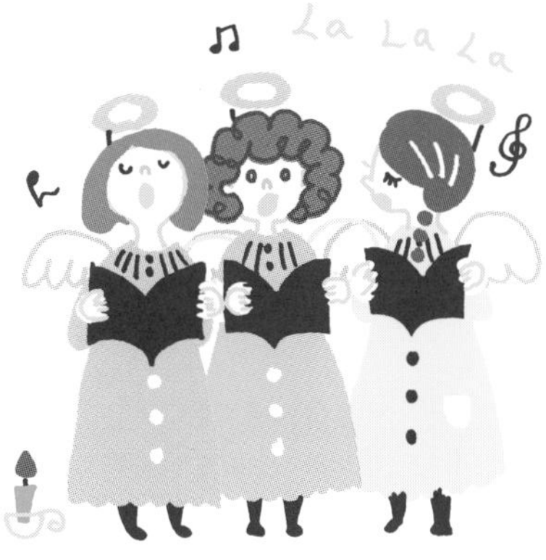
La La La

01 02 03 04 05

01 02 03 04 05

merry
cristmas

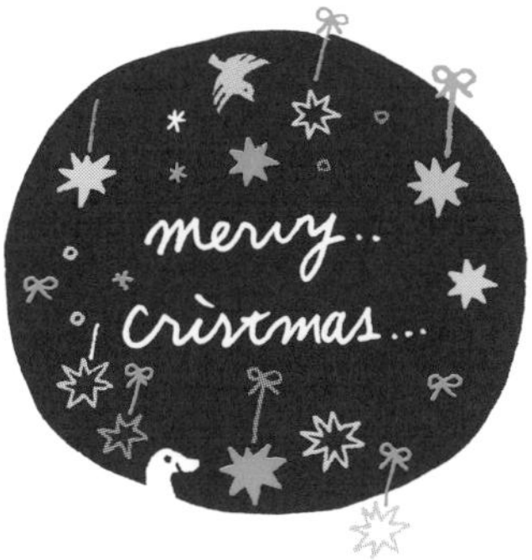
merry..
cristmas...

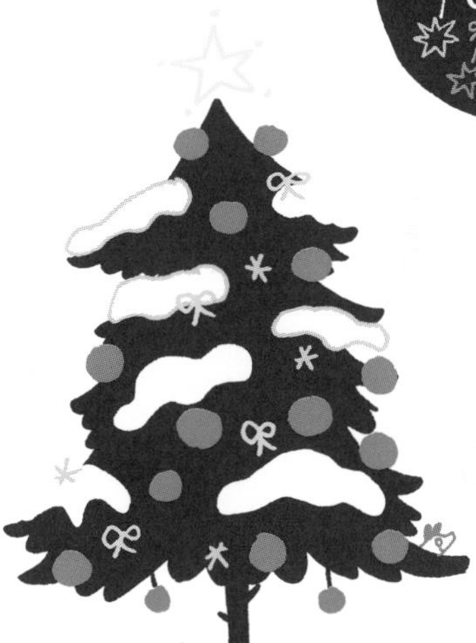

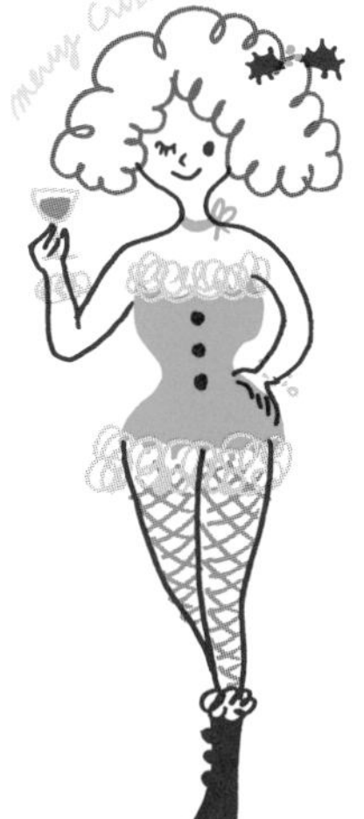
merry Cristmas!

01 02 03 04 05

01 02 03 04 05

01 02 03 04 05

01 02 03 04 05

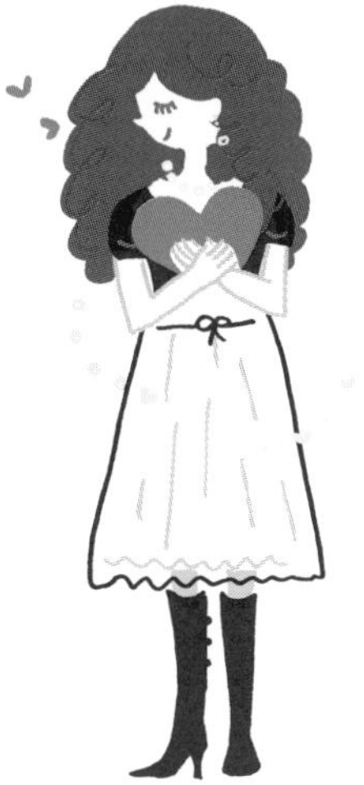

Love

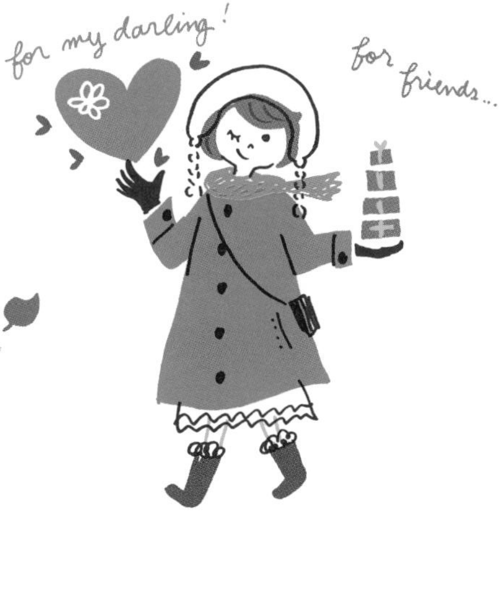
for my darling!
for friends...

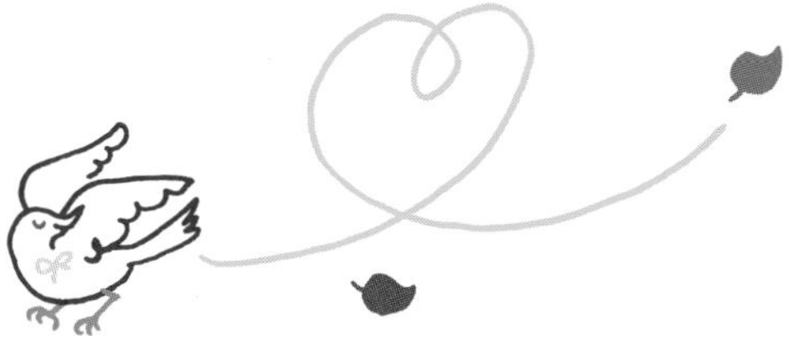

01 02 03 04 05 06

01 02 03 04

01 02 03 04

01 02 03 04

01 02 03 04

01 02 03 04

01 02

FREE STYLE SCRAPS 04
GIRLIE ガーリー

2007年9月10日 初版第1刷発行

編集・デザイン：　4D2A

イラスト：　松尾ミユキ
いとうまちこ
オカモトオモコ
eto

翻訳：　R.I.C.出版株式会社

制作進行：　石井早耶香

発行人：　安藤健一

発行所：　株式会社ビー・エヌ・エヌ新社
〒163-1111
東京都新宿区西新宿6-22-1
新宿スクエアタワー11F
Email：info@bnn.co.jp

印刷・製本：　株式会社 シナノ

Printed in Japan
ISBN 978-4-86100-534-3